A Leeds Playhouse production

*Happy
Happy
Happy*

THERE ARE NO BEGINNINGS

by Charley Miles

There Are No Beginnings was first performed as the opening
production in the Bramall Rock Void at Leeds Playhouse on
11 October 2019.

THERE ARE NO BEGINNINGS

by Charley Miles

Cast

HELEN	**Natalie Gavin**
JUNE	**Julie Hesmondhalgh**
FIONA	**Jesse Jones**
SHARON	**Tessa Parr**

Company

Director	**Amy Leach**
Set & Costume Designer	**Camilla Clarke**
Lighting Designer	**Amy Mae**
Composer & Sound Designer	**Charlotte Bickley**
Casting Director	**Nadine Rennie**
Assistant Director	**Sameena Hussain**
Trainee Assistant Director	**Shreya Patel**
Audio Description Director	**Chloë Clarke**
Audio Description Director	**Vicky Ackroyd**
Observer Director	**Anna Marshall**

Production

Company Stage Manager	**Richard Pattison**
Stage Manager	**Michelle Booth**

Cast

Natalie Gavin | HELEN

Theatre includes: *Pygmalion* (Headlong/West Yorkshire Playhouse); *Mermaid* (Shared Experience); *The Crucible* (Old Vic Theatre); *Bracken Moor* (Tricycle Theatre); *Shirley* (Hope Mill Theatre/Square Chapel). TV includes: *The English Game* (Netflix); *Ackley Bridge* (Channel 4); *Line of Duty* (BBC One); *Gentleman Jack* (BBC One/HBO); *Jericho* (ITV Studios); *The Syndicate*, *Prisoners' Wives*, *Casualty*, *The Chase* (BBC), *Shameless*, *Shameless Christmas Special* (Channel 4). Film includes: *Hector*, *The Arbor*, *Jasmine*, *The Knife that Killed Me*.

Julie Hesmondhalgh | JUNE

Julie trained at LAMDA and is best known for her award-winning portrayal of Hayley Cropper in *Coronation Street*. Theatre includes: *Mother Courage and her Children*, *The Almighty Sometimes*, *Wit* (winner of Best Female Performer 2017 MTAs), *Black Roses: The Killing of Sophie Lancaster* (winner Best Studio Performance 2012, MTAs), *Blindsided* (Manchester Royal Exchange);*The Greatest Play in the History of the World* (Edinburgh Fringe Festival/ Royal Exchange); *The Report* (Royal Court); *God Bless the Child* (Royal Court Jerwood Theatre Upstairs). TV includes: *Doctor Who*, *Catastrophe*, *Broadchurch* (BAFTA nomination for Best Supporting Actress, 2018), *Happy Valley*, *Black Roses* (RTS Award for Best Actress 2015), *Moving On*, *Inside No. 9*, *Banana*, *Cucumber*, *The Dwelling Place*, *Pat and Margaret*, *The Bill* and *Dalziel and Pascoe*. She is a speaker for Arts Emergency and founder of Take Back, an award-winning political theatre collective in Manchester. Julie's most recent films include *Pond Life* with Bill Buckhurst, and *Peterloo* directed by Mike Leigh.

Jesse Jones | FIONA

Jesse was raised in Bradford where she trained as dancer for five years before moving to London to join the LAMDA foundation course. She then went on to study on the BA Acting course at East15, where she played such roles as Annie (*Muswell Hill*), Lady Capulet (*Romeo and Juliet*) and Ariel (*The Pillowman*). While at East15 she was also the recipient of the Laurence Olivier Bursary Award. Since graduating in 2018 her credits include *Under Water Love* (Futures Theatre Company); *The Unnatural Tragedy* (The White Bear); *Bare* (Raindog Films). In her spare time Jesse is also an artist who paints abstract portraits.

Tessa Parr | SHARON

Theatre includes: *Be My Baby*, *Hamlet*, *A Christmas Carol*, *Europe*, *Road* (Leeds Playhouse); *B!RTH* (Manchester Royal Exchange); *Frogman*, *The Breakfast Plays* (Traverse Theatre, Edinburgh); *Romeo & Juliet* (West Yorkshire Playhouse); *Playdough* (Unlimited Theatre Co); *The Wonderful Wizard of Oz*, *Get Santa* (Northern Stage); *Theatre Uncut '15* (Theatre Uncut); *The Soaking of Vera Shrimp* (Live Theatre/Pleasance); *Dead To Me* (Greyscale/Kitchings Co); *Alice in Bed* (Tender Buttons); *Funny Not Funny* (Drywrite/ Bush). TV includes: *Love, Lies & Records* (Rollem Productions), *Father Brown*, *Parades End*, *Casualty 1909*, *Doctors* (BBC). Tessa is a core member of the Deaf and Hearing Ensemble, and also performs her own work as spoken word poet Johnny the Biblical Rapper.

Creative Team

Charley Miles | Writer

Charley is a playwright from rural North Yorkshire. She has written plays for the Royal Court, Paines Plough, Leeds Playhouse, and the Royal Welsh College of Music and Drama. She was attached to Paines Plough as their Playwright Fellow in 2018/19, and Leeds Playhouse as their Channel 4 Playwright in Residence in 2017. Her debut play, *Blackthorn*, was a finalist for the Susan Smith Blackburn prize in New York in 2017. Her play *Daughterhood* is currently on tour with Paines Plough. She has original television dramas in development with Participant Media, Buccaneer Media, Entertainment One and Mam Tor Productions.

Amy Leach | Director

After working across the UK for fifteen years as a freelance director and facilitator, Amy joined Leeds Playhouse in 2017 as Associate Director. Amy's directing credits at Leeds Playhouse include *Hamlet*, *Road*, *A Christmas Carol*, *Talking Heads*, *Queen of Chapeltown*, *Romeo & Juliet*, *Kes*, *The Night Before Christmas* and *Little Sure Shot*. Amy has also directed work for Hull Truck Theatre, Sherman Theatre Cardiff, National Theatre Wales, National Theatre Studio, Gagglebabble, Wales Millennium Centre, Unicorn Theatre, London, Library Theatre, Manchester, The Egg, Bath, Dukes, Lancaster and Royal Exchange Theatre, Manchester. Between 2003 & 2011, Amy co-founded and ran en masse, an award winning touring theatre company which created work for young people and their families.

Camilla Clarke | Set & Costume Designer

Camilla trained at the Royal Welsh College of Music and Drama, Graduating in 2014 with a first class BA hons degree in Theatre Design.

Designs include *Inside Bitch*, *Bad Roads* and *Human Animals* (Royal Court); *A Small Place* (Gate Theatre); *Beginners* (Unicorn Theatre); *Elephant* (Birmingham Rep); *Out of Water* (Orange Tree Theatre); *The Tide Whisperer* (National Theatre Wales); *Highway One* (August 012 & Wales Millennium Centre); *Frogman* for Curious Directive (Traverse Theatre); *Paul Bunyan*, *The Day After* (English National Opera); *Wind Resistance* (Lyceum Theatre). Other designs include *No Place For A Woman* (Theatre503); *Yuri* (Chapter, Cardiff).

Camilla was a winner of the Linbury Prize for Stage Design in 2015. Other Awards include the Lord Williams Prize for Design and The Prince of Wales Design Scholarship.

Amy Mae | Lighting Designer

Amy trained at RADA on the postgraduate Stage Electrics and Lighting Design course, and has a degree in Stage Management and Performing Arts from the University of Winchester. She won the Knight of Illumination Award for Musicals in 2015. Theatre includes: *The Playboy of the Western World* (Gaiety Theatre, Dublin); *Two Trains Running* (Royal & Derngate, Northampton); *Sweeney Todd: The Demon Barber of Fleet Street* (Harringtons Pie and Mash Shop, West End and New York); *Noises Off* (Lyric Hammersmith); *[Un]Leashed: Sense of Time* (Birmingham Royal Ballet); *The Memory of Water* (Nottingham Playhouse); *The Trick* (Bush Theatre, UK tour); *Wild East* (Young Vic, Genesis Directors Award); *Hansel and Gretel* (Rose Theatre, Kingston); *The Fishermen* (Trafalgar Studios, Edinburgh Fringe, Arcola Theatre, UK tour); *Three Sat Under the Banyan Tree* (Polka Theatre, Coventry Belgrade, UK tour); *About Leo* (Jermyn Street); *Mountains: The Dreams of Lily Kwok* (Manchester Royal Exchange, UK tour); *The Exploded Circus* (Pavilion Theatre, Worthing, UK Tour); *Br'er Cotton* (Theatre503); *Othello, Jekyll and Hyde, The Host* (NYT Rep Season 2017); *Half Breed* (Talawa at Soho Theatre and Assembly Rooms); *Start Swimming* (Young Vic/Summerhall Edinburgh); *The Ugly One* (Park Theatre); *Babette's Feast* (The Print Room); *The Lounge* (Soho Theatre); *Wordsworth* (Theatre By the Lake); *Paradise of the Assassins* (Tara Theatre); *I'm Not Here Right Now* (Paines Plough Roundabout and Soho Theatre); *Knife Edge* (Pond Restaurant, Dalston); *Prize Fights* (Royal Academy of Dramatic Art); *Orphans* (Southwark Playhouse); *Macbeth* (Italia Conti); *Liolà* (New Diorama Theatre); *Children in Uniform, Punk Rock* (Tristan Bates Theatre); *The Three Sisters* (Cockpit Theatre); *Henry V* (Royal Academy of Dramatic Art); *Pool, The Gut Girls* (Brockley Jack Theatre); *The Legacy* (The Place).

Charlotte Bickley | Composer & Sound Designer

Charlotte Bickley is a composer, sound designer and DJ. As a composer and sound designer, she has collaborated with visual artists on interactive sets and installations, such as 2017's Arctic Bazaar project, in partnership with East Street Arts and &/Or Emporium, and a touring light installation with local lighting artist Marcus Christensen. Since completing a traineeship in theatre sound design at Leeds Playhouse supported by Brighter Sound in early 2019, she's gone on to create the score and perform in Joana Nastari's award-winning *Fuck You Pay Me* at The Bunker, alongside playing live electronic sets at festivals across Europe under her alias, Carlos.

Nadine Rennie CDG | Casting Director

Nadine was in-house Casting Director at Soho Theatre for fifteen years; working on new plays by writers including Dennis Kelly, Bryony Lavery, Arinzé Kene, Philip Ridley, Laura Wade and Vicky Jones.

Since going freelance in January 2019 Nadine has worked for Arcola Theatre (*HOARD*; *The Glass Menagerie*), Tiata Fahodzi (*Good Dog*), Orange Tree Theatre (*Little Baby Jesus*), Sheffield Crucible (*The Last King of Scotland*), Fuel Theatre (*The Little Prince)* and continues to cast for Soho Theatre (*Typical*; *God's Dice*; *Shuck n Jive*).

TV work includes: BAFTA-winning CBBC series *Dixi*, casting the first three series.

Nadine also has a long-running association as Casting Director for Synergy Theatre Project and is a member of the Casting Directors' Guild.

Sameena Hussain | Assistant Director

Sameena Hussain is the Resident Assistant Director as part of the Regional Theatre Young Director Scheme. She is a theatre maker and artist based in West Yorkshire. She has worked with various theatres, arts organisations and communities. The majority of her work is rooted in community theatre; it has always been about getting to know the community, tell their stories and engaging them in creative experiences. She uses drama as a tool to engage people in creativity and play and her theatre background is in psychophysical training and ensemble work.

Credits: Directed *Henry V* (Lawrence Batley Theatre). She was the Trainee Director (JMK Trust) at the Leeds Playhouse autumn 2018: Assistant Director on *Road*, *A Christmas Carol* (Dir. Amy Leach), *Europe* (Dir. James Brining), *The Jungle Book* (Dir. Adam Sunderland) and *Jack and the Beanstalk* (Dir. Joyce Branagh).

Shreya Patel | Trainee Assistant Director

Shreya first came to Leeds Playhouse as a performer in the community production *Searching for the Heart of Leeds* in 2017. Since then she has created new work within the Playhouse's Young Company, a collective of young artists from a multitude of creative backgrounds, and discovered directing through the Intro to Directing course for D/deaf and Disabled People at the Playhouse enabled by the Regional Theatre Young Directors' Scheme. This is her first directorial role since completing the course.

Chloë Clarke | Audio Description Director

Co-founder of Elbow Room Theatre in Wales, Chloë Clarke is a visually impaired performer and director with a specialist knowledge of audio description and its creative integration into theatre. She works internationally as an Audio Description Consultant collaborating with artists, companies and organisations to improve access for visually impaired audiences in unique, innovative and exciting new ways. Her work in this field has culminated in the publication of a 'Guide to Engaging Visually Impaired Audiences', commissioned by the Arts Council of Wales.

Recent credits include National Theatre Wales, Warner Bros. Entertainment, Manchester Royal Exchange, Wales Millennium Centre, The Point and Leeds Playhouse.

She is proud to be an Audio Description Director on the premiere of *There Are No Beginnings*, which will incorporate live audio description that has been seamlessly woven into the script and sound design.

Vicky Ackroyd | Audio Description Director

Vicky Ackroyd began audio describing 10 years ago and worked to create the integrated audio description for Leeds Playhouse' production of *Road*. She regularly audio describes for a number of venues and theatre companies across the north, and has described dance, large scale outdoor performances and art exhibitions. Vicky works with lots of different creative organisations exploring accessible and inclusion.

There has been a Playhouse in Leeds for almost 50 years; from 1970 to 1990 as Leeds Playhouse, then, with the opening of a new theatre on its current Quarry Hill site it became West Yorkshire Playhouse until reclaiming its original name in 2018.

Leeds Playhouse is one of the UK's leading producing theatres; a cultural hub, a place where people gather to tell and share stories and to engage in world class theatre. It makes work which is pioneering and relevant, seeking out the best companies and artists to create inspirational theatre in the heart of Yorkshire. From large-scale spectacle to intimate performance we develop and make work for our stages, for found spaces, for touring, for schools and community centres. We create work to entertain and inspire.

As dedicated collaborators, we work regularly with other organisations from across the UK, independent producers, and some of the most distinctive, original voices in theatre today. Through our Furnace programme, we develop work with established practitioners and find, nurture and support new voices that ought to be heard. We cultivate artists by providing creative space for writers, directors, companies and individual theatre makers to refine their practice at any stage of their career.

Alongside our work for the stage we are dedicated to providing creative engagement opportunities that excite and stimulate. We build, run and sustain projects which reach out to everyone from refugee communities, to young people and students, to older communities and people with learning disabilities. At the Playhouse there is always a way to get involved.

There Are No Beginnings is the first show to be performed in the Bramall Rock Void; a versatile and exciting space for new work and an inspirational space for new artists. The creation of the Bramall Rock Void has been made possible by the long term partnership between the Liz and Terry Bramall Foundation and Leeds Playhouse. It forms part of the significant redevelopment of Leeds Playhouse, which includes a new city-facing entrance, and improved access to and around the theatre via its new foyer spaces.

Leeds Playhouse – Vital Theatre

Artistic Director **James Brining**
Executive Director **Robin Hawkes**
Chairman of the Board **Sir Rodney Brooke CBE**
Find us on Facebook: **Leeds Playhouse**
Follow us on Twitter: **@LeedsPlayhouse**
Follow us on Instagram: **@LeedsPlayhouse**

LeedsPlayhouse.org.uk

Leeds Theatre Trust Limited Charity Number 255460
VAT No. 545 4890 17 Company No. 926862, England Wales
Registered address Playhouse Square, Quarry Hill, Leeds, LS2 7UP

Supporters & Thanks

Major Funders

Capital Trust and Foundations

   The Wolfson* Foundation

BackstageTrust

   Arnold Burton Charitable Trust
R E Chadwick Trust
The Peter Black Charitable Trust

Major Donors

Sir Rodney and Dr Lady Clare Brooke

Principal Capital Partners

 MODA CaddickGroup.

Principal Capital and Access Partner

'IM' irwinmitchell

Capital Supporter

Corporate Partners

 ·GateleyPlc

Directors' Club

Gold Members

Silver Members

Bronze Members

Trusts and Grants

Project Partners

Playhouse Patrons

Platinum: Sir Rodney Brooke CBE, Dr James and Diana Drife, John Duncalfe, Charlie and Rosalind Forbes Adam, Clive & Virginia Lloyd, Anne Muers, Mr Roland Stross, Mr & Mrs J Thornton.

Gold: Neil Adleman, Ed and Heather Anderson, Mr A Blackwell, Nick and Linda Brown, Hilary Curwen, Nicola Down, Mr R Duncan, Mike Ellis, Mrs Anne Emsley, Jacqueline Harris, Gwyneth Hughes & Chris Brown DL, Sarah and Bruce Noble, Ali Rashid

For more information on how you could help to support the valuable work in our theatres, local schools and communities please contact the Development team on 0113 213 7256 or fundraising@leedsplayhouse.org.uk

Leeds Theatre Trust Limited operating as Leeds Playhouse is a not-for-profit organisation and a registered charity (number 255460).

THERE ARE NO BEGINNINGS

Charley Miles

Author's Note

This play was written for, and about, the women of Leeds –
of the 1970s and beyond. Women who have failed to be
portrayed with voice and agency, women who continue to be
underestimated and forgotten.

This is not a play about the Yorkshire Ripper, the victims of his
crimes (the claimed, the unclaimed, and those who were
attacked), or their families. But it would not be right for us to go
without remembering them: most especially, those women who
were murdered between October 1975 and January 1981.

Patricia Atkinson
Jacqueline Hill
Emily Jackson
Jean Jordan
Barbara Leach
Jayne MacDonald
Wilma McCann
Vera Millward
Yvonne Pearson
Irene Richardson
Helen Rytka
Marguerite Walls
Josephine Whitaker

C.M.

Thanks and Acknowledgements

As part of the research for this play, I interviewed dozens of brilliant and brave women, and spoke in passing to dozens more. They have made their contributions in huge, story-defining ways, and in the significant, beautiful and terrible details of everyday life. To all I have spoken to as part of this process, who have trusted me with their stories – thank you. I hope we have done your voices justice.

Thank you to Ros Goodman, whose story I could have never found from a history book or documentary.

Thank you to Elaine Benson, for her invaluable knowledge and perspective. I only hope we can begin to match your integrity in this text.

Thank you to Jalna Hanmer, whose academic work became the bedrock for this play.

I absorbed countless books, films and documentaries as part of this process: thank you for those who have done that work – most especially to the inspirational Una for *Becoming Unbecoming* and to Jalna Hanmer and Sheila Saunders for *Well-founded Fear.*

Thank you to all those in the Heydays community at Leeds Playhouse who so generously contributed their time and stories. Thank you to the women of Feminist Archive North, for their dedication and tireless energy; we stand on your shoulders.

Thank you to everyone at Leeds Playhouse who continued to support and believe in both this play and my ability to write it over my four-year struggle to do so: most especially to Gilly Roche, Jacqui Honess-Martin, James Brining and Robin Hawkes, and to all who contributed to the development process. Thanks to the Channel 4 Playwrights' Scheme, for giving me the opportunity to give this script the focus it required.

Thanks to the brilliant women of our cast and creative team, who have interrogated this play with such fierce integrity and sensitivity. Thank you Amy Leach – our director – for bringing light, warmth and joy to even the darkest places.

Thank you to my family; to my touchstone, Tashan; to my partner; and to my agent, Marnie Podos. You all keep me sure.

Thank you, Mum.

C.M.

'During the five years that the so-called Ripper roamed the North, the consciousness of women began to be transformed. Women began to call on women to depend on each other, and not men.'

Well-founded Fear, Jalna Hanmer and Sheila Saunders

Note on Play

The play should be surrounded by male voices / recordings / music. They should be pressing in on every side.

Bold, italicised stage directions are used for the voices of recordings. The audio as appears in the text has been collated from recordings from the era, but is intended as a guide only. As far as possible, sound design should feature original audio recordings.

– in place of dialogue denotes an active choice not to speak.

– between lines of dialogue denotes an unclaimed silence.

The premiere production featured integrated creative audio description to make the play fully accessible for a visually impaired audience, without the use of headsets. This was achieved in collaboration with an audio description team and the sound designer, creating a soundscape that reflected the action on stage and including the use of some stage directions as dialogue.

This text went to press before the end of rehearsals and so may differ slightly from the play as performed.

THE ACTOR PLAYING JUNE
>   There are no beginnings.
>   There are no endings.
>   When we start something we don't know that we
>   have started on it until
>   Until we are far down that road and we can
>   Look back.

THE ACTOR PLAYING FIONA
>   There are endings.
>   There's certainty in endings and
>   When something ends
>   You might not know it, here
>   But you feel it, here.

THE ACTOR PLAYING SHARON
>   These fixed points these
>   Stars connecting
>   Making patterns
>   These narratives that someone else tells
>   That makes sense of things
>   That shouldn't be made sense of.

THE ACTOR PLAYING HELEN
>   I can say where this starts.
>   I can tell you the precise
>   The exact
>   The very fucking moment.

THE ACTOR PLAYING FIONA
>   I could take you right onto the
>   Edge
>   The tip
>   Of the knife that drives into the heart of it.

THE ACTOR PLAYING SHARON
>   I could make sense.
>   I could
>   I could make sense of it all
>   If I wanted to.

THE ACTOR PLAYING JUNE

> There are no real beginnings but here's one:
> Rain.
> Can you hear it?

THE ACTOR PLAYING SHARON

> A street wi' houses. Red-brick. Most the lights
> already out.

THE ACTOR PLAYING HELEN

> A dark night.

THE ACTOR PLAYING FIONA

> A dark and stormy night.
> Like that?

THE ACTOR PLAYING HELEN

> And a park.
> A sort of park but not one wi' pretty flowers and
> benches. Just grass.
> The kind of park you might not want to cross by
> yourself
> At night

THE ACTOR PLAYING SHARON

> In the dark.
> That row of houses just over there.
> See them?

THE ACTOR PLAYING FIONA

> Some kids waiting in that house
> That one right there in the middle.

THE ACTOR PLAYING JUNE

> Waiting for their mum to come home.

THE ACTOR PLAYING HELEN

> They'll sit. Cuddled up. Waiting till round five
> tomorrow morning.

THE ACTOR PLAYING SHARON

> Till fog creeps over the fields.

THE ACTOR PLAYING JUNE

> Like the weather knows what's happening.

THE ACTOR PLAYING FIONA
>They'll try and find her
>them kids.

THE ACTOR PLAYING SHARON
>Hands held, in a row.

THE ACTOR PLAYING HELEN
>Little links in a broken chain.

THE ACTOR PLAYING JUNE
>Thank God they never do.

>–

THE ACTOR PLAYING SHARON
>There's no such thing as beginnings
>there's just

THE ACTOR PLAYING HELEN
>You know what happens next.

THE ACTOR PLAYING FIONA
>A song plays

THE ACTOR PLAYING JUNE
>And we
>Begin

>*'Crime of the Century' by Supertramp.*

>*They change their clothes:*

>FIONA, *into a police uniform*

>SHARON, *into school uniform*

>JUNE, *into a blouse, a skirt, a pinny.*

>HELEN *changes into a bridesmaid dress.*

>*Pink, with Bo-Peep frills.*
>*A 1980s triumph.*

>*She feels like a*
>*fucking*
>*goddess.*

>*The vinyl judders.*

In Leeds.

HELEN prances; she twirls.
Has this girl ever twirled before in her whole life?

The vinyl skips.

In the red-light area of Leeds.

She caresses the dress
like it's the most precious silk.

The body of a woman

And suddenly
She can't stand it on her skin a second longer.

The body of a mother

She tears it off.
Rips it off.
Drags it off.

The body of a prostitute

And she feels our gaze very keenly.

Has been found murdered

She steps into the bath
like it's by rote.
Like it's the only thing she knows to do.
Like it's the thing she's destined to do
again
and again
and again.

She's submerged.

The music stops. Or does it come to an end?

ACT ONE

OCTOBER, 1975

HELEN *explodes from the water.*

JUNE *watches.*

HELEN	The hell d'you think you're doing??
JUNE	You've still got your undies on love. Can't get clean with our undies on now can we?
HELEN	Get out!!
JUNE	I just need to do a once-over of you before we get you settled.
HELEN	Stop fucking looking!!
JUNE	I'm sorry love, but when we've had our little look we can give you a nice big dinner. Cuppa tea. What d'you say.
HELEN	Dyke.
JUNE	– Stand up Ellen. Tek your knickers off. There's a girl.
HELEN	That's not my name. My name's Helen. With an 'H'.
JUNE	Sorry. Helen.
HELEN	Like out of Troy.
JUNE	Like what now?
HELEN	My mum saw a film.
JUNE	It's a good name Helen.

HELEN   –

JUNE   I know it's a little strange, in't it.
            I've just to check you've nothing on you.

HELEN   On me??

JUNE   Can't have you bringing owt in now can we.

HELEN   I promise.

JUNE   Just a quick twirl around.
            Like a fashion show, ey?

SHARON   Mum?

HELEN   I promise on my life.

JUNE   On your life's a big one Helen.
            Best just give us a twirl, there we go.

            It pivots on a breath –

SHARON   Mum?

JUNE   I'm a little busy love.

SHARON   But you're always busy these days aren't you
            Mum.

JUNE   Sharon…

SHARON   Dad wants to know what time you're home.

JUNE   I'm not sure.

SHARON   Dad wants to know what's for tea.

JUNE   There's shepherd's pie in the fridge.

SHARON   But that's what we had last night.

JUNE   Sharon

SHARON   And the night before.

JUNE   I'm busy, Sharon.

SHARON   Yeah.

FIONA   Name's Helen Harker.

SHARON   We know you are.

It pivots on a breath –

FIONA   First-timer. Fourteen years old.

JUNE   Family?

FIONA   Mum's in the nick. Dad's
             We don't have a dad on record.
             She's been living with auntie and uncle past few
             months but seems things have got a bit fractious
             at home.

JUNE   The problem is
             This is a one-off and we're full so
             Is there no way we can get her back home tonight?

FIONA   Even if she was keen
             Which she isn't
             The aunt's had enough of her.
             I think *he'd* have her back. If I'm honest.
             Between you and me, I get the impression she's
             better off out of there.

JUNE   We're full. I dunno what to say to you.

FIONA   The uncle
             Summat not right there, if you catch my drift.

JUNE   Did you mention that? About the uncle?

FIONA   It's just an instinct.

JUNE   Tell them that.
             They like instincts, your lot, don't they?
             That's what they say in the pictures.

FIONA   It's not instinct they like, it's gut. And not very
             attractive for us to have a gut is it?

JUNE   Very good.
             I don't think we've crossed paths before.

FIONA   PC Bainbridge.

JUNE   You're very young...
             June.
             Mrs Collier to them.

             –

FIONA   Fiona.
               When I'm not on duty.

JUNE   It's nice to meet you Fiona.
               Hope I'll be seeing more of you.
               Good to have some female company for a change.

FIONA   I don't want her out on the streets tonight. There
               nowt you can do?

JUNE   We've not got a bed for her.

FIONA   What with the murder.

JUNE   What murder?

SHARON   'Scuse me

JUNE   Round here?

FIONA   Yeah. Another silly girl.
               Just like her.

SHARON   'Scuse me.

JUNE   Round Chapeltown?

               It pivots on a breath –

FIONA   Park's closed.

SHARON   My friend lives just across there.

FIONA   Where?

SHARON   Down Scott Hall Grove.

FIONA   You can get round on the road.

SHARON   But

FIONA   You can go round to get to Grove.

SHARON   But
               I'm dressed up…

FIONA   –

SHARON   I want to take the short cut 'cross the park.

FIONA   Well you can't.

SHARON   –
What's happened?

FIONA   An accident.

SHARON   What sort of an accident?

FIONA   A murder.

SHARON   Wow.
Alright…
Fine…
I thought you were in a costume d'you know.
I was coming up to tell you it was well good in't
that funny?

FIONA   –

SHARON   Don't see a lot of woman police, do you.
Do you like it?
In't it scary?

FIONA   You can go round by the road. It won't take you
ten minutes longer.
And no. I don't get scared.

SHARON   Not even when there's a murder? On Halloween?
That's a bit scary in't it. That's really creepy.
Why'd you do that on Halloween, ey? It's like you
really really trying to freak people out. Was it an
accident, actually?
Or was it like a proper stabby thing?
Like an actual, intentional, you know
Bloody hell. Creeping myself out now.
It's really dark. I can't believe you've gotta stand
here on your own.

FIONA   I'm not on my own.

SHARON   I can't stay for long.
I wouldn't've thought they'd let a lady p'liceman
on her own.

FIONA   My colleague's just round there.

SHARON   Oh right.
Still. I think you're dead brave. Even if he is just

round the corner.
Your colleague, I mean.

FIONA   It's my job to not get scared.

SHARON   I'm a dead bride.
          Good in't it?

FIONA   –

SHARON   Alright well
          Thanks
          P'licelady.

FIONA   Bainbridge.

SHARON   What?

FIONA   That's what you're supposed to call me.
          It's PC Bainbridge.
          Not 'P'licelady'...

Vinyl
scratches.
Comes to the end of a record.
A deep thud.

In Leeds, the body of a woman has been found brutally

The track skips

Brutally
Brutally
Brutally
Brutally
Brutally

A record plays.
'Too Young' by Donny Osmond.

SHARON   Mum?
          Daaaddd?
          Can you heeeear me?
          I don't think you're iiiiiiiinnnnn?

          She listens –
          then turns the music up.

She grabs a magazine
furtively.
Starts reading.
Gets more in to it.
She grabs a pillow and puts it between her legs.

JUNE   Sharon?

SHARON   I'm not!

JUNE   –
            What you doing?

SHARON   I'm just
            I'm not
            You know I am fifteen years old you cannot come
            barging into my bedroom whenever you please
            and
            I have got rights you know.

JUNE   I thought you were going to Sue's Halloween
            thing.

SHARON   Someone's got murdered near her house so

JUNE   It was near Sue's house?

SHARON   Yeah.

JUNE   –

SHARON   I wasn't feeling well.

JUNE   Hey?

SHARON   Why I'm in my bedroom.
            Were you not even gonna ask?
            I thought you were at work.

JUNE   I am. I've a favour to ask you.

SHARON   Alright fine if I can have a hot chocolate…

JUNE   Hot chocolate?
            When you're feeling sick?

SHARON   –

JUNE   You don't even know what the favour is yet.

SHARON   Have I got a choice?

JUNE   –

There's a young girl needs a bed for the night.

SHARON   What?

JUNE   She's very near your age.

SHARON   What sort of young girl?

JUNE   We've run out of space at the unit.

SHARON   MUM.
What are my FRIENDS going to say??

JUNE   They're going to say
what a sympathetic and lovely young girl that
Sharon Collier is.
Helping out someone so in need.

SHARON   That is not what anyone says ever.

JUNE   Sharon please.
She's a very young girl and I know that it's not
It's just one night.
You're not gonna send that poor little girl back out
onto the street are you? After that horrible thing
that's happened.

SHARON   –

I spoke to the police about it.

JUNE   You what?

SHARON   I saw the police where it happened.

JUNE   Christ Sharon. Gave me a fright for a minute.

SHARON   Why?

JUNE   Thought you'd seen something or

SHARON   Well obviously not

JUNE   The way you said it.

SHARON   Happened in the middle of the night when I was at
home asleep.

	Not like you're gonna go murdering at teatime are you.
JUNE	Sharon...
SHARON	What? You're not. That's the way you come home though. After you're on nights.
JUNE	–
SHARON	Well that's a bit creepy in't it.
JUNE	Stop it. What's wrong with you.
SHARON	Just watching out for you Mother. – She's not having my bed.
HELEN	Hi.
JUNE	I'm sure she's had worse than Crossley carpet.
HELEN	Hi.
	It pivots on a breath –
SHARON	Hi.
	–
SHARON	Sharon.
HELEN	Yeah.
SHARON	– I dunno your name.
HELEN	It's Helen. This your bedroom?
SHARON	Well obviously.
HELEN	Didn't realise.
SHARON	What?
HELEN	When she said home thought she meant like Summat social or summat. But this is her house, is it?

SHARON   –
           It's our house.

HELEN   She your mum?

SHARON   No she's just some total stranger lives in same
           house as me...

HELEN   –
           You're funny.

SHARON   –

HELEN   What's that?

SHARON   Hot chocolate.
           What you never had hot chocolate before?

HELEN   What's that in it?

SHARON   Thermometer?
           You never had your temperature taken before?

HELEN   –
           You gonna drink that?

SHARON   Yes.
           It's my treat for
           –
           Look I'm sure she'd make you one if you ask.
           I'm sure she'd make you a bloody ocean of hot
           chocolate and let you swim round in it if you ask.

HELEN   God. An ocean of chocolate...
           Can you imagine that?

SHARON   –
           Yes.
           –
           Look I am gonna drink it. I'm just
           I probably shouldn't tell you. Because you're
           probably quite unreliable.

HELEN   I am not unreliable.

SHARON   Well

HELEN   I'm probably one of the most reliable persons you
           ever met before in your life.

SHARON   Well I don't know you do I.

HELEN   So what d'you go around calling people unreliable
           when you ent got a clue about a person.

SHARON   I know you go to the place where my mum
           works at.

HELEN   So?

SHARON   And that kinda says a lot about the kinda person
           that you are.

HELEN   It does not.

SHARON   And sometimes in life you just have to make
           a quick assumption about a person.

HELEN   My quick assumption is that you are a cow.

SHARON   I will tell
           My mother
           What you just said.

HELEN   I'll tell her about your thermo-whatsit.

SHARON   BUGGER!

HELEN   What?

SHARON   Nothing.
           –

           Look I've not been very welcoming have I so here

HELEN   Really?

SHARON   Yeah.
           Drink up.

           –

HELEN   Thanks...

SHARON   Wait! Jesus Christ are you some kind of idiot?
           You can't drink that.

HELEN   What?

SHARON   The thermometer – it cracked.
           It's got mercury in it stupid. It'll poison you dead.

HELEN   You trying to kill me??

SHARON   No it was a
           Bloody joke, wasn't it.
           I didn't actually think you'd be stupid enough to
           drink it…

HELEN   I'm not stupid.

SHARON   Well I didn't mean that / you're

HELEN   I am not fucking stupid alright?!

SHARON   Yeah. Alright.

HELEN   As if I even want to be here in your stupid
           frilly curtains and shit.
           Fucking
           Donny Osmond.

SHARON   Excuse me

HELEN   Who likes Donny Osmond??

SHARON   Everybody likes Donny Osmond.

HELEN   No one does.

SHARON   He's universal.

HELEN   He's what?

SHARON   He's not just a pop star you know he's got good
           morals and everything.

HELEN   Yeah and you'd know about morals and that
           wouldn't you.

SHARON   –

HELEN   Cos you're so
           all of this.

SHARON   I don't

HELEN   Think you're so
           fucking Lady.

SHARON   I don't.

HELEN   You are.

          –

SHARON   Well
          I spose I'm sorry
          If that's how I come across.

HELEN   It is.

          –

SHARON   I'm actually quite nice.

HELEN   –

SHARON   You can put your bag down, if you like.

HELEN   –

SHARON   Is that all your stuff in there?

HELEN   For now.

SHARON   It must be really hard.

HELEN   What?

SHARON   You know.

HELEN   What?

SHARON   –
          D'you like music?
          I'm really into my music.

HELEN   –

SHARON   D'you want to see my records?

HELEN   Can do.

SHARON   I've got a load from my mum and dad that are bit
          shit but
          this lot's all mine. From birthdays and Christmas
          and dentists and
          you know
          pocket money and stuff.

HELEN   Dentists?

SHARON   So who's your favourite?

HELEN   Dunno.

SHARON   Those one's are all Progressive.

HELEN   What?

SHARON   I actually dunt know what it means.
But it says it look
See?
Says it there on the sleeve.

HELEN   Oh yeah... Yeah I see.

SHARON   So them ones all live together. Got a really precise system. Always know when Dad's been rifling through.

    –

SHARON   D'you like my mum then?

HELEN   She's alright.

SHARON   She's a right pain.

HELEN   D'you think?

SHARON   She's always nagging.
    –
What's yours like?

HELEN   –

SHARON   I mean your mum.

HELEN   She's the best.
She's the best mum.

SHARON   Wow. I don't know anyone thinks that about their mum.

HELEN   She's just busy.

SHARON   Okay.

HELEN   That's why I aren't staying with her.

SHARON   Alright.

HELEN   I stay wi' my boyfriend but
          we had a tiff so
          that's when they brung me in.

SHARON   You've got a boyfriend?

HELEN   Yeh.

SHARON   What's he like?

HELEN   Nice. He buys me stuff. Nice clothes and food
          and that.
          He bought me this top.

SHARON   That is... nice.
          –
          You live with him then? Your boyfriend?

HELEN   Mostly I actually live with me auntie and uncle
          But my auntie kicked me out.

SHARON   That's horrible.

HELEN   Yeah.

SHARON   Poor you.

HELEN   –

SHARON   That one's Supertramp.
          I love them. They're really
          cerebral.

HELEN   Hey?

SHARON   Supertramp. The band.

HELEN   Sounds like something my Auntie Angela'd
          call me.
          Super Tramp.
          (*Laughs.*)

SHARON   (*After a moment
          laughs.*)

          –

SHARON   D'you want to listen?

HELEN   Go on then.

> *'Dreamer' by Supertramp*
> *on the turntable.*

> *The girls listen*
> *together.*

> *The music is infectious.*
> SHARON*'s head bobs.*
> HELEN*'s shoulders twitch.*

> SHARON *stands*
> *and starts to dance.*
> *She mimes along: grabs a hairbrush.*

> HELEN*'s embarrassed*
> *and then bemused*
> *and then amused.*

> *She joins in.*

> *The girls dance together.*
> *They fly around the room.*

> *The track sticks:*
> **Dream dream dream dream**
> **Dream dream dream dream**
> **Dream dream dream dream**

> *White noise:*
> *A radio*
> *in and out of being tuned.*

> *The signal skirts the song*
> *until we land on a broadcast,*
> *broken and patchy:*

> **In**
> **In**
> **In Leeds**
> **In leeds the b**
> **B**
> **B**
> **Body of a woman has been found**
> **Br**

Br
Br
Brutally murdered.
The third in a series of
Grrrrrrrrruuuuuuuuuuuuesome
Attacks on
Call
Call
Call girls in the region
Police renew the hunt for the man who has come to be known
as:

The Yorkshire Ripper.

1976–1977

SHARON *upgrades her look:*
trades school uniform for ruffles and platforms,
straight out of Saturday Night Fever.

JUNE *changes into a skirt, a shirt, a lanyard around her neck.*
She positions it with pride.

HELEN *swaps her skirt for a pair of jeans*
she rips the knee, scuffs the hems.

FIONA *changes her shirt*
buttons it all the way up to her chin.
Rolls a pair of stockings very carefully
but efficiently
up her legs.

There has to be a moment,
when we're changing clothes,
in which we're kind of naked.
In that moment, do they see each other?
Do they see us?

Quick –
cover it up.

ACT TWO

JUNE   What the hell you wearing.

SHARON   What???

JUNE   What on earth Sharon.

SHARON   What??

JUNE   Where did you get those, ey?
Whose are they?

SHARON   They're mine!

JUNE   And what lorry did they fall off?

SHARON   Dad give me the money for them.

JUNE   Your dad gave you?

SHARON   Yeah.
Cos he loves me.
And he wants me to be happy.

JUNE   –
Your father did not pay for those.

SHARON   Yeah he did.

JUNE   Your dad

SHARON   What?

JUNE   Where did you get the money for those ridiculous
shoes?

SHARON   My dad what?

            –

JUNE   I will not have you lie to me Sharon.
Children should not lie to their parents.

SHARON   (*Makes a noise.*)

JUNE   Excuse me?

SHARON   –

JUNE   You can head back up to your room if you're
            gonna be like that.

SHARON   You said I could go to Sue's before the stupid
            social thing.

JUNE   And now I'm saying you can head on upstairs and
            have a think about your behaviour.

SHARON   Such a joke…

JUNE   What's that?

SHARON   I said:
            This is such a joke.

JUNE   We'll be talking about this when your father's
            home.

SHARON   D'you not mean when you're home?
            Cos it's you that's never home Mum.

JUNE   Just go and get changed.

SHARON   Why you so bothered about what I'm wearing?

JUNE   Cos you look

SHARON   Like a what?
            Like a pro?

FIONA   A pro.

JUNE   Don't you use that word.

SHARON   Just want to fit in don't I.

FIONA   Sometimes, you know.

JUNE   You know sometimes
            Sometimes I wonder where I went so wrong
            wi' you.
            When you can be such a nasty little girl.

FIONA   You know sometimes you can be

SHARON   Sometimes you can be such a BITCH.

           It pivots on a breath –

FIONA   Sometimes you can be very difficult to work with
           June.

JUNE   Me?
           Is that meant to be funny?

FIONA   Obstructive.
           You're not going to stop me from charging her.
           You literally cannot stop me from charging her.

JUNE   This is what happens though in't it.
           We try and tell you lot this is exactly what'd
           happen.
           You have no respect for what we do here.

FIONA   You lot?

JUNE   How old are you?

FIONA   Excuse me?

JUNE   I must be old enough to be your mother.

FIONA   Well you're not my mother.
           –
           I thought we were getting friendly.

JUNE   Friendly listens to friend.
           And I told you. We told you, months back now
           We don't want it. The girls don't want it.

FIONA   This is the third time in a fortnight June. I can't do
           her favours on account of your special
           relationship.

JUNE   What you talking about special relationship I treat
           'em all exactly the same.

FIONA   (*Makes a noise.*)
           –

JUNE   Thrice in a fortnight?
           D'you not see? It's happening exactly as we said
           it would.

	She's getting worse because of what you lot have done.

FIONA   It's not 'us lot' that've done it!
          It wasn't legal. You're not police, you're not
          a hospital

JUNE   No we're a damn sight better than both those.

FIONA   You can't keep 'em locked up! You can't restrain
          'em.
          Where's your training for that? Show me your
          qualifications?
          It wasn't right.

JUNE   So let me just get this crystal clear now so we're
          both on the same page. So your version of this is:
          They come in. We clean 'em up, help 'em out,
          keep 'em safe.
          And then let 'em wander right back out onto the
          streets again?

FIONA   You encourage them to remain in a safe space. If
          you're doing your job as well as you say you are,
          they wouldn't even want to leave.

JUNE   So they wander back out onto street. Where they
          get in trouble. Again.
          And end up in a police cell this time.
          And then that's where you can *legally* lock
          'em up.

FIONA   You know it's not as simple as that.

JUNE   With a record to boot, now.

FIONA   You're a smart woman.

JUNE   Bloody listen to us then!

FIONA   It's for her own good.

JUNE   You're giving that girl a criminal record!

FIONA   Got to be something stops her doing it.

JUNE   You think that's the way to stop her?

FIONA   We do what we can.
               Don't we.

JUNE   Yes. We do.

               –

FIONA   I am your superior you know.

JUNE   Love, please.
               We both know that's not the way it works.
               Might be the way it works wi' your lads in the
               office.
               But look at who you're talking to.
               –
               You know he sits out there that
               bloke of hers. That
               Pimp she thinks her boyfriend. He sits out there in
               his car
               And before, nowt she could do but twitch curtains.
               Oh and she'd be effing and blinding at me – I've
               gotta see my boyfriend, this and that.
               You can't lock me up.
               She had this
               They all have this
               This little performance they play out.
               And they're the damsel in the tower and I'm the
               mean old witch and him out there in his Cortina,
               Prince Charming. Come to rescue.
               We'd play out our little scene, just loud enough so
               he can hear.
               Mean old witch here wins again.
               Prince Charming. Off he drives.
               On to try another
               Princess.
               And then the damsel and the hag sit down for
               a nice cuppa and though she dunt say it
               That girl's glad for every brick in this ivory tower.
               And what have you lot done?
               You've come and driven a bulldozer through the
               bloody wall.

FIONA   Would you stop it with the 'you lot' please.

JUNE	I'll stop it when you finally get a mind of your own Fiona love. How old are you?
FIONA	And stop calling me love.
JUNE	Still at home I'm betting.
FIONA	You are so unprofessional.
JUNE	You don't know what it is to take care of a person. And them lot are teaching you totally the wrong way to go about it.
FIONA	It's not my job taking care of people.
JUNE	...Exactly.
FIONA	I know how the world works just as good as you. Don't go off on me because you never got the chance to do summat bigger.
JUNE	Bigger?
FIONA	Don't get me wrong – you do a good job at doing what you do. But don't be going off at me because you got yourself saddled with a husband and a mortgage and one too few O levels.

–

| FIONA | I'm taking Helen down station now.
Gonna give her some motivation to start changing her life.
I honestly think it'll do more than a cuppa tea.
I honestly do believe that cos |

–

| | I didn't ever once look at a policeman and think I can't do that.
Even though you'd think that a girl like me
that looks like me
That that'd be the last thing in the world I'd believe that I could do.
Could be.
But that's why I do know, June. I know the way that girl's brain ticks. I know about hard choices. |

And I know about pulling yourself up by bootstraps.
Cos you try being a PC on the streets of
Chapeltown in 1975.
You try being me
on the beat on the streets of Chapeltown, in them
riots.
Wearing two uniforms.
Cuddles don't get us anywhere at end of day. They
might feel warm and nice but you're still left
standing right there in same spot at the end of it.
Whereas a good kick up the arse
Might land you on the ground for a minute
But you get back up again. And when you do,
you're stood in a different place than where you
started.
You're further forward. You've moved on.
We want the same thing. We do. We just got
different
methodology.
She'll thank me for it, sooner or later. You wait
and see, one day
When that girl is grown up and got herself sorted
out
She'll thank me for doing this.

JUNE   (*Laughs.*)

FIONA   ?

JUNE   I'm sorry, Fiona love, but that's where you're very
            wrong indeed,
            cos you ent never getting any thanks out of that girl.
            Kicks, cuddles, whatever you want to say.
            You're still here thinking you're gonna be the
            hero.
            On your white horse. Into the sunset.
            But we're not the heroes. We're not Prince
            Charming come to rescue.

SHARON   She is such a

JUNE   We're the mean old witch.

SHARON   SUCH a

JUNE	That's how *we* save the day.
	It pivots on a breath –
SHARON	SUCH a BITCH! She has absolutely no respect for me. She's got more respect for *you*.
HELEN	Like your shoes.
SHARON	You can have 'em.
HELEN	Seriously??
SHARON	You can try 'em on…

–

SHARON	She thinks I'm such an idiot.
HELEN	They are well high.
SHARON	Does she honestly think I can't even read??
HELEN	What? You can't read?
SHARON	Of course I can bloody well read! I mean my mum. As if she has the nerve to go on about *me* lying to *her* when she's not even telling me about my own dad.
HELEN	What about your dad?
SHARON	That they're closing down the mill. He's gonna lose his job. That's why they're being so URGH. Parents… And it's been all over the bloody papers.
HELEN	D'you actually read the papers?
SHARON	Not actually. Someone at school told me. But still. I could. If I wanted to.

–

| SHARON | So when's this social kicking off? |

HELEN	Social?
SHARON	Biscuits and cola...
HELEN	The party?
SHARON	Yeah.
HELEN	Why you call it social?
SHARON	It's what my mum calls it. Cos I told her – it's not really a party, is it. A party's got music and dancing and Boys.
HELEN	We'll have music.
SHARON	Crap music.
HELEN	Why you come then if it's so crap?
SHARON	Mum likes me to come as like you know kind of as like a Good Example.
HELEN	–
SHARON	Does that sound a bit bad?
HELEN	Nah it's alright. I get it.
SHARON	You seen the pictures of *Saturday Night Fever*? In the mags? They're like out of that. John Travolta, in that film, is a Sex. God.
HELEN	Your dad really get you these?
SHARON	Nah. Course not. I got 'em off my friend Sue. Her brother's into well dodgy stuff. I reckon he probably nicked 'em. I reckon he probably fancies me.
HELEN	My boyfriend buys me stuff. Get to see him all the time now. Now they can't lock us in.
SHARON	Helen can I ask you about...

HELEN   What?

SHARON   About.
           You know.

HELEN   You know… what?

SHARON   About…
           (*Sex!!! – mouthed? Gestured? Never said.*)

HELEN   Oh.

SHARON   Is that alright?

HELEN   Um yeah. Suppose.

SHARON   You have
           (*Sex!!!*)
           right? Like, all the time.

HELEN   What d'you mean by that?

SHARON   Just like

HELEN   What you asking for?

SHARON   I saw this thing in the papers the other day. Like
           I was actually reading about that other girl that got
           killed you know
           But then opposite I saw this bit about Mae West,
           you know the film star? She's proper old-school.

HELEN   Never heard of her.

SHARON   'Hollywood Pays Tribute to Sex Queen'. Here
           actually look I

           Fetches a paper.

           See? Papers.

           Points to a line in the paper.

HELEN   –
           What about it?

SHARON   Look at that bit. There.

HELEN   –
           –

SHARON   See? That bit.

HELEN   So?

SHARON   So you're not... that's not... surprising. To you.

HELEN   –

SHARON   I don't want to be offensive.

HELEN   –

SHARON   I just want to know what's normal.

HELEN   Normal about what?

SHARON   Like I was surprised that she lost her
          you know
          at thirteen years old. Thirteen. That's really young,
          right?!

HELEN   –

SHARON   (*As Mae West.*)
          'Not been without a man for more than a week
          since then.'

HELEN   I mean that's not hard.

SHARON   Is it
          really good?

HELEN   S'alright. Sometimes.

SHARON   I really want to be normal.

HELEN   Don't get what you mean when you say that.

SHARON   I'm worried everyone's doing it and I'm not.

HELEN   –
          You shouldn't do stuff just cos other people are
          doing it Sharon. That's a really silly reason to be
          doing stuff especially stuff like that
          cos you know it can be like
          Yeah it can be like really nice and actually like
          There's times you really want it. But you know
          sometimes
          Even if you think you really want it, sometimes
          you have it

And it's not like what you think it's gonna be like.
Like it's not always kissing and
Like don't get me wrong sometimes it is, it's
really good but sometimes
Sometimes when I'm doing it, I've started it, so
I can't like go back on what I've started, obviously
But I suddenly realise right in the middle that
I really really don't want to be
There. And like all my whole body tenses up and
I start feeling a bit sick and every single
movement, every single like
Each one of those just makes me feel more and
more
And more and more like I'm not a person any more.
Like I'm not really
Real
any more.
And then I have to just think about like
blue skies
or summat.
–
So if you want my advice I'd say
Just don't start to do summat unless you're one
million per cent sure because you can't go back on
summat once you've started.

SHARON   You can't?

HELEN   No. You can't.
            –
            Look, you better take these back.

SHARON   Nah it's alright, you can wear them for a bit. If you
            like them.

HELEN   Think they're taking me in to the station so
            Should probably tek 'em back.

SHARON   Police station?
            Are you in trouble?

HELEN   There's this one woman got it in for me.
            She just sits there in her car all fucking day
            waiting for me.

SHARON   What d'you mean?

HELEN   She dunt like my boyfriend.
She just sits there waiting for me to
Like
Any time I go anywhere near

SHARON   What?

HELEN   Like I can't even have a bloody conversation
without her breathing down me neck. Think she'd
have better stuff to do right.

SHARON   Yeah.

HELEN   What with them murders and that.
Think she'd have better stuff to be doing than
stalking me.

SHARON   Yeah.
You scared, Helen?

HELEN   Of what?

SHARON   You know, when you're out and about.

HELEN   Dunno. Not really.
Mebbe when it's dark, a bit.

SHARON   Last night, when I was walking home from school,
there was this car drove past and this man stuck
his head out the window and yelled 'You looking
for Jack tonight? Why don't you come with me
instead.'
It's getting really weird round here, in't it.

Radio fades up.
A bulletin:

With the time now at five fifty-nine
here's the mid-evening news on BBC
BBC
BBC 2
with Peeeeeeeeter Woods.

The body of a young woman has been found murdered
MurMurMurdered

Murdered
in the playground of a
Leeds suburb early this morning.
Another in a series of gruesome
Gruesome
attacks that had, until now, focused on prostitutes.

The Yorkshire Ripper's fifth victim has been
identified as
an innocent, sixteen-year-old shop assistant.

an innocent, sixteen-year-old shop assistant.

an innocent, sixteen-year-old

an innocent.

We bring you more after the headlines.

SHARON	Jesus. Mum. That's
FIONA	Jesus. That girl. That poor girl.
JUNE	Jesus. That poor girl. Her poor parents.
HELEN	Poor her.
SHARON	She's not She wasn't a She's just a girl
JUNE	She was a beautiful girl. Always smiling. Her poor parents.
FIONA	Must've been a
HELEN	Poor lass.
SHARON	Was it a mistake??
JUNE	She wasn't a

FIONA   Where was she walking?

JUNE   Was she alone?

SHARON   What were she wearing?

HELEN   Poor her.

FIONA   What the hell was she wearing?

JUNE   That poor girl. Her poor parents.

SHARON   To mek him think

FIONA   What the hell was she doing walking that way by
           herself?

JUNE   At that time of night?

SHARON   Jesus Mum it's
           Jesus Mum.
           It's

JUNE   He must of thought

FIONA   What the hell was she wearing to mek him think
           she was

JUNE   She wasn't a

FIONA   She wasn't

SHARON   She was just

FIONA   Who's safe now?

JUNE   No one's safe now.

SHARON   Am I not safe now??

HELEN   Am I not safe now?

FIONA   No one's safe now.

           –

FIONA   You must all stay aware. Walk in twos.
           Keep your eyes out for each other.
           After it gets dark, then stay put.
           Unless it's dark where you are, in which case
           Find somewhere light.

Don't draw attention to yourselves.
If you hear something suspicious
Speak up.
We're always listening.
If you hear someone behind you
Speed up.
Cross the road.
Knock on the door
Of a well-lit house.
Avoid public transport after dark.
Find alternatives.
Stick to the paths you know best
Don't stray from your well-trodden routes.
Get home or find a phonebox.
Maintain communication.
Telephone home before you set off home.
Tell someone to expect you.
Telephone a neighbour before you leave for home.
Leave a message.
Keep a look-out.
If you get the feeling you're being followed
Don't panic.
Slow down.
Let him pass
So he's in front of you and not behind.
Don't worry about offending Them.
Keep an eye out
Keep a note on
Keep a mental snapshot
Of key physical features
Of any man you might suspect.
Scar?
Tattoo?
Facial hair?
Height? Weight?
What was he wearing?
Where was he heading?
As well as the time and the place.
Don't go home with men you don't know.
If you suspect someone
Speak up.

Talk to a teacher or to a friend.
Listen to your friends.
Listen to your fathers.
Listen on your friends and your fathers.
Check your back seats
before you get in your cars.
Write down this phone number.
Call us with information.
Personal safety alarms will be issued
By County Council.
Avoid the sites of previous crime scenes.
Avoid quiet areas.
Avoid areas known for soliciting
and the pubs and places nearby.
Avoid dark streets.
Avoid ginnels.
Avoid men.
Don't go out after dark.
Don't go out alone.
–

And don't worry.
We'll catch him soon.

It pivots on a breath –

SHARON   They said not to worry though.
          They said they're catching him soon.

HELEN   But what else were they saying?

SHARON   She kept trying to make like weird jokes. Like she
          was our mate.
          'Now's not the time to be looking for a new
          boyfriend, ladieeeees!
          Stick with the one you've got for now – wink
          wink.
          And get him to walk you home from school.'
          So. Embarrassing.

HELEN   They said that in front of teachers and all?

SHARON   They called a girls-only assembly for it.

HELEN   Can I see your alarm?

SHARON   It's totally useless.

HELEN   Dunt work?

SHARON   Works fine but my mate Sue used hers the other
          day
          It was fine she wasn't actually in trouble she just
          got nervy and set it off by accident. But no one
          came.

HELEN   What no one come to help her?

SHARON   No one knows what the noise means.
          You've got to know what the sound means for it to
          do any good.

          –

SHARON   Look at her face on the telly.

HELEN   She's pretty.

SHARON   I knew her, Helen.
          I mean I'm like not gonna pretend we were best
          mates or owt but we were in Brownies together.
          She was my sixer.
          We were
          Kelpies.

HELEN   ?

SHARON   They picked a good picture.
          Not that she isn't
          you know
          not that she wasn't pretty.

HELEN   Funny way to get on the telly.

SHARON   I wish they wouldn't have it on all the time.
          It's like every time I turn it on and there she is.
          I don't want to think about it
          all the time.
          Like obviously I want to remember her and that's
          Important
          But I don't want to think about
          that
          all the time.

HELEN   I always thought that if I were ever on the telly
            it'd be cos I was a famous actress or summat.
            Or that I'd done summat good and I was on *Blue
            Peter.*

SHARON   But it's probably better that it's actually on all the
            time. Cos it means that they're like proper trying,
            aren't they. They're really set to get him now.

HELEN   Yeah. It'll make a difference this will.
            That's what everyone's saying.

SHARON   –
            Sorry.

HELEN   What?

SHARON   Hadn't really thought about it till now but
            Kind of makes it different, doesn't it.

HELEN   It does yeah.
            People really didn't give much of a shit when they
            thought he were just after pros which is
            It's pretty bad that actually, in't it.

SHARON   God yeah it's awful.
            I'm sorry. I'm
            So sorry. On behalf of like
            Of us all.

HELEN   –
            What?

SHARON   Of everyone who's not one
            On behalf of them. Us.

HELEN   What you sorry for?

SHARON   That people didn't care so much
            or not that they didn't care but
            felt like when you're watching the news about
            starving kids in Africa. And you're seeing them
            big swollen bellies and flies going in their eyes
            and I'll be honest
            Sometimes I even cry seeing that stuff on the telly.
            It's awful.

And my dad says I'm really sensitive and stuff
when I do but
I hadn't even though this before but
Like it's really sad.
So I could be sad about it but then also like
not really sad.
Cos sometimes it's nice to feel sad about them
things. And then you feel a bit good about having
felt a bit sad.

HELEN   Yeah I get what you mean.

SHARON   So I'm sorry that I
That we
That I didn't have the full sympathy for you.
Before.
Empathy I guess that is. In't it. That's the
difference.

HELEN   –
What?

SHARON   Prostitutes were like the starving children in
Africa. To me.

HELEN   Empathy?

SHARON   It's different to sympathy cos
I learnt about it in English the other day
It's the difference of having feelings, and sharing
feelings.
And I definitely didn't share before. With you.

HELEN   Are you saying I'm a pro?

SHARON   –
What?

HELEN   You think I'm a pro?

SHARON   Um.

HELEN   Why d'you think I'm a pro?

SHARON   I thought

HELEN   It's not like that.

SHARON   Oh my god Helen

HELEN   You thought I'm a pro this whole time??

SHARON   I am so sorry.

HELEN   Why d'you think that?

SHARON   I dunno I think I just thought
You know cos like most the girls my mum works
with

HELEN   Not all the girls. Not me.

SHARON   Oh my god

HELEN   I mean like
That's not what I am.
I'm not an actual pro.

SHARON   I'm so sorry. It's just the way you talked about it
sometimes.

HELEN   Like what?

SHARON   Like about
Like about your... boyfriend. His mates.

HELEN   Yeah but it's different, it's not
It's like sometimes I get myself into a bit of
a situation wi' money, and you've gotta pay
people back right? We're not all
Daddy's little princess.

SHARON   Well there's no need / to be

HELEN   And like, that's just a way to get the money. To pay
'em back.
Like sometimes I just have to pay him back
His mates back
and sometimes I get away with just doing
something else
instead.

SHARON   Yeah, course. That makes sense.

HELEN   It's just the odd fiver here and there.

SHARON   I get it now.

HELEN   –

SHARON   I'm really sorry Helen.

HELEN   Yeah.

SHARON   I had no idea that…

HELEN   Yeah well I spose maybe I get why you could've
             thought that.

SHARON   Yeah it's just a messy probably
             Grey area.

HELEN   He loves me, my boyfriend.

SHARON   Course he does.

HELEN   Just sometimes

SHARON   What about the bruises though?

HELEN   He gets a bit overexcited. Or
             like I'm sure we can all agree I can get a bit out of
             hand, can't I.

SHARON   –

HELEN   D'you think…?

SHARON   Maybe you should talk to my mum about all this.

HELEN   –

SHARON   She'd probably be a lot better than me.

HELEN   God
             You must think I'm a right fucking idiot.

SHARON   Not really.

HELEN   I just never really thought about it like that before,
             you know? In't it odd all the things you can do
             and actually just not properly think about. But I'm
             thinking now back over all the
             Yeah. You're probably right Sharon.
             I suppose I am one.
             –
             Funny that.

–
You're pretty smart, you are.

SHARON   I'm not really.

HELEN   Smarter than me.

SHARON   I'm not even that good in school.

HELEN   I don't even go school.

SHARON   My mum's always saying no one'd ever give me
a job.

HELEN   Better than having a job and not even knowing it,
ey?

SHARON   –

HELEN   Better than doing all that and being summat and
giving all your money to someone and not even
knowing that you're doing it.

SHARON   I don't think that's your fault.

HELEN   Whose fault is it?

SHARON   –

HELEN   Nah it's a good thing, in't it. It's a good thing
I know now or that
You know that I realise properly what I am. Cos
it's not who I am, is it. It is just what I am. Cos
you can be a builder or a teacher. Can't you?

SHARON   Yeah. Yeah you can be a teacher.

HELEN   In't it funny what happens without you realising it?

SHARON   What d'you mean?

HELEN   Like it's happened before, it has.
Like when I was at home with my mum and my
sisters, and then all of a sudden I was living with
my auntie and uncle. And I'd been living there for
like a year, only I hadn't even realised it until
I had this massive blow-out row with Angela, my
auntie, and she says that I've been living under her
roof for a year and don't I have any gratitude.

A year, she said
You've been living under myyyyyy roof for
a YEAR young lady!!

–

Took a sec for it to sink in cos I hadn't even
realised.
It'd just gone week by week, in my head.
I had to pull myself up and think for a minute, and
think –
Yeah. Actually. I have been living here for a year.
Probably should be grateful to her, for that.
But at the time I was always, I was just always
thinking that my mum was away for a bit. But
that's how temporary stuff becomes forever,
I suppose.
Happens without you ever noticing it.

SHARON   It's really shitty, Helen.

HELEN   What is?

SHARON   It's not fair, the life you've got.

HELEN   We've got what we've got, haven't we.

SHARON   But it's not fair, is it.

HELEN   Least I'm not her, ey.
That's not fair, is it.
At least I'm not dead.

–

SHARON   So what you going to do?

HELEN   Dunno.
Negotiate better terms, probably.

1977–1978

Sirens.
Fizz and crackle of radio static.
Angry music.

SHARON *wipes tears from her face,*
replaces them with mascara.

JUNE *swaps her skirt for a pair of jeans.*

FIONA *changes frantically between shifts*
She doesn't have any clean underwear
So she turns the ones she's already wearing inside out.

HELEN *dresses in reflective white: head to toe.*

He obviously has an intimate
An innnnnnnnnntimate knowledge
of the centres of towns and cities within West Yorkshire.
He obviously spends quite some time in those towns and cities
and for various other reasons I feel that
I feel that
I feel I feel I feel
He lives with us
Or very close to us
Or works with us
With with with with with us.

Obviously now any woman out alone at night must be
considered at-risk.
And police advise
Police would advise
That women should not go out at night unaccompanied.

And police advise
Police would advise
That women should not go out at night unaccompanied.

And police advise
That women should not go out at night unaccompanied.

Women should not go out at night unaccompanied.

ACT THREE

FIONA	Have you got someone you'd like to call?
HELEN	Where's my stuff?
FIONA	Sister, friend.
HELEN	Want my stuff back.
FIONA	They'll bring your effects down in a minute.
HELEN	Better not be owt missing.
FIONA	Helen. Pay attention. Is there anyone you'd like to call to come get you?
HELEN	I don't trust anyone, me. Just cos you've got uniforms dunt mean not a one of yous got sticky fingers. I had a fiver in my purse.
FIONA	Helen – the phone.
HELEN	Don't need it.
FIONA	Maybe you can call Mrs Collier at the unit.
HELEN	I'm gonna walk.
FIONA	Where?
HELEN	None of your business.
FIONA	It's my business to make sure you stay safe.
HELEN	(*Makes a noise.*)
FIONA	What?
HELEN	Nothing.
FIONA	What's that noise for?
HELEN	Safe?

FIONA	Safe.
HELEN	Know what's safe? Pocket full of cash.
FIONA	Not the way you go about earning it.
HELEN	How else d'you expect me to earn it when you go about arresting me.
FIONA	There are other ways.
HELEN	With a record?
FIONA	Clean a floor. A toilet.
HELEN	Think people want a cleaner they think's dirty? You ent got a clue. You lot.
FIONA	– I can call Mrs Collier for you if you'd like.
HELEN	Said I'm alright.
FIONA	I can dial the number. If that's what you're worried about.
SHARON	Helen?
HELEN	Piss off. I wanna walk.
JUNE	Where do you think you're off to?
	It pivots on a breath –
SHARON	Helen I had this dream last night, right. And it felt like mad real.
JUNE	I'm not having you get the bus. It's not safe. Not on your own.
SHARON	I was walking by myself at night down the road
JUNE	A taxi? With what money?
SHARON	And I sort of knew, in the dream, already, that it was already a dream cos there's no way in hell I'd be walking around by myself at night, right.

JUNE   You'll have to wait till your dad's home. Maybe
              he can take you.

SHARON   So it was like that weird sort of – knowing you're
              sort of dreaming, but also not knowing it.

JUNE   I don't have the time to be escorting you around
              madam!

SHARON   So I'm walking down the street and suddenly
              there's someone behind me. And I just know, right
              away, it's him. Right? You just know, yeah. No
              one else around. Pitch black. Hearing his
              footsteps.

JUNE   If you open that door

SHARON   I walk a bit quicker and he walks a bit quicker and
              my heart is pounding like it's gonna push right out
              my chest and then flop on the pavement.

JUNE   Alright – you head and get yourself killed then!

SHARON   And he hits me. Like with all the others. I feel it
              right in the back of my head like a
              You know, a hammer. Right back there. And I turn
              around to see him
              But it's my mum. And she's holding a hairbrush
              and even though I'm in the street, when I turn
              round she's in my bedroom and she's obviously
              been brushing my hair like I'm a little girl again
              and she says 'No pain without gain, Sharon.'
              But that's not right, is it? It's – no gain without
              pain, right? Should be.
              Went on for ages. Facing forwards and it's like
              I'm being attacked in the street, and when I turn
              around I'm having me hair brushed.
              What the hell's that all about, ey??

JUNE   You go and do
              whatever the hell you like.

              It pivots on a breath –

HELEN   I don't have dreams.

SHARON   What d'you mean you don't have dreams?

HELEN   Not even nightmares.

SHARON   God that's so weird.
           –

           Look I wanted to say
           Will you meet me tonight?
           Will you meet me on North Street after dark?
           There's something happening tonight Helen and
           I just feel
           I feel like it's important we be there. Both of us.
           Me and
           You, especially.

HELEN   You alright?

SHARON   I'm angry. You should be too.
           You've got more to be angry about than most.

HELEN   You alright?

           It pivots on a breath –

           I said: you alright
           Mrs Collier?

JUNE   Helen. Sorry. I didn't see you there.

HELEN   I'm quiet, me. Stealthy. Like a spy.

JUNE   That you are.

HELEN   People's always saying they're never hearing me
           come up on them.

JUNE   Are they now.

HELEN   Make a good Ripper wouldn't I?

JUNE   –

HELEN   Was just a joke.

JUNE   I don't think that's very funny do you.
           What you in for today?

HELEN   Got my check-in and gonna stick around for
           dinner.

JUNE	Alright.
HELEN	Seeing Sharon later.
JUNE	Sharon's going out later?
HELEN	Ahhh I thought
JUNE	— You've got summat on your top there.
HELEN	Ah yeah…
JUNE	Should be more careful wearing white. Shows the dirt. You want a change?
HELEN	Nah it's alright. I'm off to work. Don't reckon a bit of red sauce'll put 'em off.
	—
JUNE	Have you got your Durex?
HELEN	Course I have.
	—
HELEN	When I said I'm seeing Sharon later Like obviously I'm seeing her Before I head out.
JUNE	—
HELEN	Have I made you worried? Don't worry Mrs Collier. I wouldn't worry. She's alright. I mean I'm out most nights and I've never seen him so You know it's probably that you're more afraid cos you don't ever go out by yourself any more. Just being driven around everywhere by Mr Collier and that's probably mostly why you're so scared. Cos it's only one bloke, in't it. He can't be everywhere. It's actually pretty good odds you're not gonna run into him. You know my mum used to be dead scared of mice and then we lived in this flat that had a shitload of

mice in it and then after a while – she wasn't even
scared any more.
She'd be sleeping on the sofa and they'd run right
over her like she were a little mouse road and
hardly even notice.
Call it 'exposure therapy', that.

JUNE   You're still out most nights Helen?

HELEN   I didn't mean to get in to all that.

JUNE   I don't think it's quite like exposure therapy.

HELEN   It's not as bad as you think you know. We do look
out for each other.
If someone's not back in twenty
We watch out for each other. And we've got a rule
right.
You seen all them photos in the papers? He's got
a beard, right. So we're all just not going with any
beardies.
Almost feel sorry for 'em. All the beardies of
Leeds and none of them are getting any.

JUNE   Jesus Helen. How can I

HELEN   Are you crying? Don't cry.
The beard thing, meant to be a bit funny.

JUNE   How can I persuade you to stop?

HELEN   I'm fine. Look at me. Head's in one piece and all!
If you could ever say that about my head, ey.

JUNE   Why will you not just listen to us??

HELEN   I do listen.

JUNE   How can you expect me to keep you safe when
you're determined to make the worst choices.

HELEN   Yeah alright

JUNE   Where are you going Helen?? Come back here.

HELEN   I don't come here to get shouted at alright.
I know I'm a piece a shit. Fair dos maybe I'll get
got next.
Don't need you making me feel worse about it.

JUNE   Helen. Helen! You get back in this house.

HELEN   I'm not your fucking daughter!

FIONA   Are you alright?

HELEN   I'm fine!!

FIONA   Are you alright?

SHARON   I'm fine. I'm fine.

FIONA   Are you alright?

JUNE   I'm fine. I'm just

            It pivots on a breath –

FIONA   Doesn't seem like you're fine. Should I come back?

JUNE   I'm fine. I'm just
            having a bit of a day of it.

FIONA   Fine fine fine.
            Hear that word so much stopped knowing what it
            means, you know?
            Finefinefinefinefine…
            –

JUNE   I am
            –
            I am
            fine. Honest.
            It's just not a good time to have a teenager.

FIONA   Specially not a unit full.

JUNE   Actually it's my own giving me most gyp right
            now.

FIONA   I didn't know you had a kid.

JUNE   You must've known that.

FIONA   Sort of assumed that's why

JUNE   What?

FIONA   That was why you do this. Cos you couldn't have
            one of your own.

JUNE   You thought that?

FIONA   You just never mentioned a kid.

JUNE   In all these years? You must've forgot.

FIONA   I think it's just never come up.

JUNE   She must have.

FIONA   Daughter? How old?
            Teenager, did you say?

JUNE   I don't believe I haven't mentioned her to you.

FIONA   Well it's not like we're friends.

            –

FIONA   We're more like colleagues, is all I mean.

            –

FIONA   So how old is she?

JUNE   Seventeen.

FIONA   That's bad timing. For now.
            I sometimes think though that be better – to have
            the worry of a girl, than a boy.

JUNE   I'm petrified every time she steps foot out the
            door.
            Can't decide if it's worse for her to be getting on
            empty buses or walking.
            We can't afford taxis to be ferrying her round but
            even if we could
            I mean I'd never let her get in a taxi, these days.

FIONA   Would you not?

JUNE   Bloody hell. Course not.

FIONA   What about your husband? In't he in taxis these
            days?

JUNE   Dennis in't a taxi driver he's just
            driving taxis, for now.

            –

JUNE   She does netball on a Wednesday night.
          Coach says they're only allowed to go once
          everyone's got their lift.
          So they're there all lined up outside sports hall
          like a little battalion.
          Causes a nightmare of traffic but it's only when all
          the dads are there that a single one of them gets in
          a car.
          Couldn't have imagined that, when I was a girl.
          Can you imagine not being allowed to walk home?
          As a seventeen-year-old?

FIONA   But I'd rather worry about a daughter than having
          to think my son could be out there doing people in.
          Cos he's gonna be someone's son, in't he.

JUNE   –
          I'd not thought about it like that.

FIONA   Spose that's what you get happening to your head
          when you spend your days going door to door,
          hoping to chat to a serial killer.

JUNE   Can you believe that it's one man doing this to us?

FIONA   I have thought that, at times.

JUNE   One man.
          One little man.
          One pathetic boy.
          All this.

          –

FIONA   I've some new photofits to ask the girls about.

JUNE   How d'you want to do it? One by one or all
          together?

FIONA   She got away, this one. It's not been in the
          papers yet.

JUNE   Well that's… good. In't it.

FIONA   It is.

JUNE   Nice to have some good news, for once.

FIONA   –

JUNE   –
           You still knocking on then?

FIONA   Like a bloody milkman.

JUNE   You'll find him soon.
           I have faith.

FIONA   Do you?
           That's nice to hear.
           Not many people saying that these days. Just feels
           like
           Feels like a lot of blind alleys. Can be a bit
           disheartening. But they've started a new team
           now. Dedicated unit. Calling it the Ripper Squad.

JUNE   Sounds like a pop band.

FIONA   Better than what it was called to start with.

JUNE   What's that?

FIONA   'Special Homicide Investigation Team'.
           They had to take the nameplate off the door.

JUNE   Because...

FIONA   –
           SHIT Squad.

JUNE   (*Laughs.*)

FIONA   You can take the lads out of the playground...

JUNE   So you're doing that now are you?

FIONA   Oh no. Not me. There's only twelve of them on it.
           My um
           My Robbie's doing it though.

JUNE   Your husband is he?

FIONA   Not um
           Not quite my

JUNE   Your chap.

FIONA   Yeah. My chap.
          –
          It's just a bit
          Can be a complicated with work.

JUNE   A lot of girls find their fellas at work. Nowt wrong
          wi' that.

FIONA   Yeah and then they get married and disappear.

JUNE   Disappear?

FIONA   You know what I mean.
          I want to be the first female detective in West
          Yorkshire CID.

JUNE   Wow.

FIONA   I don't want him to

JUNE   Distract you?

FIONA   He could never distract me.
          It's more that I don't want other people to
          be distracted *from* me.

JUNE   You think having a lad makes you look less
          serious?

FIONA   Yeah. I think it does.

JUNE   You're allowed a boyfriend Fiona.

FIONA   I know.

JUNE   You need to have a life as well.

FIONA   I do have a life.

JUNE   And it is nice, you know
          To have someone take care of you a bit.

FIONA   Oh yeah cos you lot all make that look so
          appealing.
          –

FIONA   Sorry.
          That was

JUNE   I'll not deny my Dennis has had his ups and downs.

FIONA   It's not my business.

         –

FIONA   I know a few lads that got laid off.

JUNE   It was a big mill.

FIONA   They shouldn't be able to just do that.

JUNE   Well no they shouldn't. But unfortunately I feel like there's probably worse to come round here in that regard.
         We're not exactly top priority. Are we.

         –

JUNE   Good on your Robbie though. Getting onto that Ripper Squad.
         Smart move, the police. Job for life there.

FIONA   I was a bit
         Tell you truth I was raging. He's not half as

JUNE   Dedicated?

FIONA   Good. He's not half as good as me.

JUNE   You are good. You're very good with the girls.
         Got a way about you.

FIONA   It's like they think I've not got the stomach for it.
         You know, I asked for that promotion.
         It's a bloody stupid
         'Scuse my language
         It's a stupid name but
         I should be on that squad.
         I actually went and asked for it! Went and asked for a meeting with the DCS.
         What a laugh he must've had.
         But there's no one my rank that's put in more hours.
         I've made three recommendations for further questioning and they've all been escalated, been taken seriously.
         But me? As if they'd ever take me seriously.

JUNE   I'm sure they do.

FIONA   They don't.
             You know when I was a cadet, few years back
             Silly little seventeen-year-old but even then
             Even then I knew how it was. Rules of the game.
             I have always played by the rules.
             They used to go out after training. There was
             a pub nearby and we'd all go there
             You know and they encouraged it even. Bonding.
             It's important in something like the force.
             You've got to feel backed up. Part of a team.
             There was only three of us lasses in that class and
             I always insisted
             Orange juice for me.
             Them other two, they were knocking 'em back
             with the lads.
             Having a jolly old time of it
             'Bonding.'
             But you know who's lasted?
             Me.
             Because there's different rules for men and women.
             And the sooner you figure that out the better off
             you are.
             Faster you'll rise.

JUNE   Do you believe that?

FIONA   Yes I believe that.
             –
             Only
             I know I'm not really rising yet but
             They will notice. Eventually.
             We just have to you know
             Do it all twice as good. Three times's fast.
             Hundred per cent more innovative. But that's what
             you do in't it.
             Risk my neck every day
             My head, I should say, every day
             Just to stay out from behind a desk.
             –
             D'you know, we're meant to be in twos? When we
             go door-knocking. We're meant to have a partner,
             that's procedure.

But we're so stretched, aren't we.
So I turn up at houses, any time of the day, by
myself, and knock on, and interview whoever's
in there.
And there's always a moment when I'm on that
doorstep and I think – this could be him.
Could be him with his hammer other side of that
door.
And then what would I do?

JUNE That sounds very scary.

FIONA They've had to reinforce the floor at Millgarth.
The ceiling. They've had to bring in workmen to
Because of the weight of the
Cos of all the paperwork
The records
The filing.
The number plates and photofits and the
transcripts and the interviews.
Just so much
Paper. You know?
The floor starting to
The ceiling started to
–
I thought it was all in my head at first.
I thought I was imagining it. That the ceiling was
coming down on me.
That the whole building was
bulging. Buckling.
–
But turns out
Wasn't just in my head.

JUNE That sounds very scary.

FIONA Most of the time I'm terrified.
But they mustn't ever know it.

JUNE That sounds very scary.

HELEN Most of the time I'm terrified.
But they wouldn't ever know it.

JUNE That sounds very scary.

SHARON   I'm not scared.

FIONA   Are you alright?

JUNE   That sounds very

SHARON   I'm not scared.

FIONA   I didn't ask if you were scared.

           It pivots on a breath –

SHARON   Well I'm alright thanks.
           Helen? Helen! Over here!

HELEN   What's this all about?

SHARON   It's a protest.

HELEN   A what?

SHARON   Like a march. Like a… like a raising of voices!
           Like a mob. A riot.

HELEN   A fucking riot?

SHARON   It's an official thing. Look this leaflet

HELEN   You gonna get me arrested.

SHARON   Of course we won't be. Don't be stupid.
           People are allowed to be on a street. People are
           allowed to like
           It's not illegal to just walk down a street.

HELEN   –

SHARON   Is it.

HELEN   –
           Never seen so many women in a place.

SHARON   Yeah it's mad in't it. Like a football match.

HELEN   Like the opposite of a football match.

SHARON   Look at that placard!

HELEN   What?

SHARON   The sign! Look at the sign she's holding!

HELEN   Can't. It's too dark.

SHARON   It's not that dark. Look, read it!!

HELEN   Fuck off I've bad eyes.

SHARON   It's that Marilyn Monroe song –
             Men grow bald, as they grow old, they all lose
             their charms in the end. All men are wankers said
             Christabel Pankhurst

HELEN   What it actually says 'wankers' on it?

SHARON   Women are a girl's best friend!!
             In't it brilliant??

HELEN   Your mum'll go mental at you being out like this.

SHARON   Did you not see the papers?
             They're trying to put a curfew on us. Police saying
             that we shouldn't be allowed out after like eight
             o'clock. After it's dark.

HELEN   You're not allowed out after dark anyway.

SHARON   But it's not US they should be putting the curfew
             on is it??

HELEN   What you talking about?

SHARON   It's MEN they should be putting the curfew on,
             isn't it??
             Think about that. Like
             There's a man going round killing women.
             And it's the women that them lot say shouldn't be
             allowed out.
             Can you not like
             When I think about that I feel summat in my chest.
             I feel like I wanna cry.
             Like I wanna scream.
             Like I wanna scream and cry at the same time.

HELEN   (*Laughs at her.*)

SHARON   You've gotta find your anger Helen.

HELEN   Alright.

SHARON   I feel like I'm learning something integral about
           myself.

HELEN   Yeah?

SHARON   I think I'm going to be a feminist when I get to
           university.

Sound starts.
Swells.
Singing. Shouting.

Men Off the Streets!
Men Off the Streets!
Men Off the Streets!

JUNE *switches on her TV set.*
Puts her feet up.

In the wake of another brutal murder
Murrrrrrrrder
MURDER
On Murder night

FIONA *patrols the fringes of the march.*

On
Murder
Murder
Monday night

SHARON *and* HELEN *in the midst of the march.*
Singing
Shouting
Throwing leaflets into the air.

SHARON   What were YOU doing on Monday night??

HELEN   What was you doing on Monday night, ey?!

But the women against violence turned violent themselves
Turned violent themselves
The women against
The violent
Turns violence

SHARON   Women demand the right
           To walk the streets at night!

> *Angry wooooooooooooo*
> *Angry*
> *Angry Angry Amgry*
> *W W W W W*
> *Angry Angry Angry Angry*
> *Angry women*

HELEN   What was you doing on Monday night?
        What was YOU doing on Monday night, ey??

SHARON Men off the streets!
        MEN OFF THE STREETS
        MEN OFF THE STREETS!!!!

> *Angry Women*
> *battle police in two-hour march*
> *In a*
> *In a*
> *Two-hour maaaaaarrrrrch through the city.*

HELEN   All men are WANKERS
        Said Christabel PANK-ERST!
        WOMEN are

> *The angry women against*
> *The violence*
> *The violent women*
> *Turn against*
> *The angry women turn violent.*

SHARON However we dress! Wherever we go!
        No means no means no MEANS NO!!

HELEN   WHAT WAS YOU DOING ON MONDAY
        NIGHT?????

> *Night getting darker.*
> *Shouts getting louder.*
> *Passion growing to fury.*

SHARON All men are WANKERS

> JUNE *turns off the TV.*

HELEN   All men are WANKERS
        Said Christabel PANK-ERST

The volume fades.
The street lights dim.

FIONA *clocks off.*

WOMEN are a

And SHARON *goes home.*

(*Singing.*) Women are

In the wake of the furore
In the detritus of the march
It seems like HELEN *is the last man standing on the*
streets of Leeds.

Women are a girl's best friend…

Blackout.

1978–1979

Music

The vinyl is scratched
It jumps and splutters

Brutal killer
Brutal killer
Brutal killer
Of at least
eight
eight
eight
women.

JUNE, SHARON, FIONA, *and* HELEN *change their clothes.*

Several recordings intersect and overlap:

The body was found in the grounds of the Manchester Royal
Infirmary at around eight
eight
eight o'clock this morning

The body was dragged through here and placed between this
pile of wood and this wall.

At about quarter to ten
ten
ten this morning police were called to a house which is known
as 'Claremont' in New Street at Farsley

found dead in undergrowth near a supermarket in the Leeds
suburb of Headingly yesterday

It's a large detached house standing in its own grounds owned
by a local mill owner. Mr Peter Wainsworth. He occupies that
house.

And in the grounds a search was made and we found, first of
all, a pair of ladies' shoes and we have subsequently found a

How did he kill her?

Died of blows to the head and stab wounds to the stomach.

sustained multiple injuries

She had blows to the head and at the same time mutilations on the body.

The body was in fact naked and it is a woman.

This is now the headquarters of Britain's biggest murder hunt.

There are a quarter of a million
a million
millon
quarter of a million files here alone.

A total of seven
seven
seven prostitutes
and one
one
one
one
one innocent girl of sixteen
sixteen
sixteen
have been found murdered.

detectives denied she was a victim of the Ripper

immediately the police saw a link with the ripper killings

Now at the press conference the phrase 'novel methods of enquiry' was used. Could you enlighten us on what that means?

Now, they've changed their minds.

I could, clearly, but I don't wish to.

That's as much as I can say at this stage.

Britain's most dangerous psychopath has indeed struck again.

ACT FOUR

JUNE   I'm not much used to grand speeches but
When it's called for! And it really is.
Called for. Today.
Who knows where she gets it from, all those
A levels!
So now you're off, abandoning your old dad and
Me.
What we gonna do without you.
Your records night and day! Dirty socks on
bathroom floor!
I'm only teasing...
–

Who would've thought that a daughter of mine
would be going to a university? First kid on this
street
No don't shush me!
Everyone's pleased for you.
Course you think a lot about this day when you're
a mother. The day your chick flies the nest.
–

That's not true.
Be honest I've barely thought it at all, all these
eighteen years.
But this is what you're meant to say, in't it.
–

Honestly there was a time
At one time I believed I'd never see the back
of you.
Six weeks old and screaming wi' colic and
I thought I'd have that voice in my head whole
rest of my life, nonstop. Whether that be plain old
crying, crying over boys or crying for help wi'
your own littl'uns.
Didn't think you'd get as far as Beeston let alone
Bradford.

And if I'm honest
Sharon
Now
I feel sick when I think of you leaving.
And I can't decide if that's because I'm jealous
or afraid.

–

I keep having dreams about you. Dreams where
you were never born. Dreams where you're just
gone.
I get these dreams where the phone's just ringing
and ringing and I won't answer it cos I already
know what the call's gonna say.
One night I woke up and the phone was actually
ringing.
And it was only work but
God my heart.
I went to watch you sleeping in your bed.
You were only just there – just sleeping in
your bed
But I couldn't stop crying.
Called into work and I'm meant to be heading out
the door and I'm standing there at your bedroom
like there's a tap turned on in my head
I had no idea I had so many tears in me.

–

I dreamt the other night that you were just as you
are 'cept in a pram again. That beautiful big old
Silver Cross your father found me from the ad in
the paper. The one I'd push you round town in as
a baby. Proud as punch, like lady of the manor.
You always were a sweet thing to look at.
I'm pushing you in the pram and I look away for
just a second, and when I turn back
you're gone. And
I just know you've been taken.
That he's taken you.
I know it very deep down inside me. In a place
that's always been there but I never knew existed
till this moment.
I think it must be the place we keep our fear.

Where we keep it till we need it most.
To keep it from overwhelming us.
I think we must be born with that place already
inside us.
And what can I do?
Empty pram.
You're already gone.

–

–

We're so very proud of you Sharon.
What a thrill for us. Look at you – sailing off!
Flying so high!
Proud as punch, aren't we Dennis.

–

There's a bottle of Asti on the table. Someone
open it!

–

To new beginnings…

SHARON   Cheers.

JUNE   Just stay safe, won't you?

              It pivots on a breath –

FIONA   And she's staying safe, is she?

JUNE   Well they've got their precautions in place now.
              Lads on all the buses to escort them to lectures
              and back.

FIONA   Maybe better teach them how to swing an arm
              rather than hang on one.

JUNE   And they're allowed their boyfriends to stay,
              overnight. In their halls.

FIONA   Since when's that a precaution?
              What's it gonna be next?
              Little generation boom from the university girls of
              the Ripper years?

              This tickles JUNE.

JUNE   Little generation of
              ?

More than she'd expect.

FIONA   They're all gonna come out crying 'men off the streets!'

JUNE   Oh don't. Enough!

Almost crying now.

FIONA   Bit of a joke in't it. Men off the streets please. But let's get them in our bedrooms – quick!

From laughter.

–

FIONA   Your husband in?

JUNE   I've not laughed like that in a long while.
Our Dennis? He's out working.

FIONA   How's he doing with all that?

JUNE   Bloody miserable sod.
I thought it might get better. After Sharon left.
Thought it might be like the old days.

FIONA   And what was he like in the old days?

JUNE   Before we had her.
Nights out at the pictures.
Shag on the sofa.

FIONA   –

JUNE   Sorry. Don't know where that came from.

FIONA   That's fine.

JUNE   I sometimes forget.
Sorry love
Here I am talking to you about my marriage. You don't want to hear about all that.

FIONA   I've been meaning to ask you about Dennis anyway.

JUNE   You're very perceptive. I think that's what makes you such a very good policewoman.

FIONA   Oh

JUNE I think since Sharon left I've been feeling a little
Lonely.

FIONA –
I'm sure that's normal…

JUNE It's like I'm speaking a different language these
days.
–
Sharon's godmother. My best friend from school.
I've spoken more wi' you over the past year.

FIONA We've all been very busy.
With work.

JUNE Bumped into her in market last week with her
grandkids
She called me a career woman.
'Oh but your Auntie June's a *career woman* now.'
And the way she said it.

FIONA People don't like you being better than them.

JUNE I don't think I'm better than anyone.

FIONA Your daughter's just gone off to university.
You don't have to do owt differently but they'll
see you different.
You'll make them feel different, just by fact of
being.

JUNE That's not what I want.

FIONA It's alright for Sharon. She's off and out.
You're the one that gets left behind.

JUNE –
It'll get better.
Must work on my small talk.
You know there was a time I could've talked about
a teabag for an hour but now
I don't seem to have the stomach for it any more.

FIONA How's Dennis feeling about all this?

JUNE I wouldn't know.

FIONA	He still in the taxi?
JUNE	Still in the taxi.
FIONA	How far out does he go in that then?
JUNE	Depends, dunt it.
FIONA	How long are his shifts?
JUNE	Varies. Why d'you ask? – Fiona. – What's all this about?
FIONA	We're asking everyone questions.
JUNE	So you're asking these questions as…
FIONA	– Well I am on-duty.
JUNE	Jesus Christ Fiona. What the hell is wrong wi' you?
FIONA	This is a favour.
JUNE	What is?
FIONA	Talking to you. First. It's a courtesy.
JUNE	– You've been asking me about my marriage.
FIONA	You just started talking about that. I never asked about any of that.
JUNE	You were asking about my husband!
FIONA	As a police officer.
JUNE	And not as a friend?
FIONA	I'm in uniform aren't I?
JUNE	If you've got something to say You say it now.

FIONA   –

JUNE   My husband is not the fucking Yorkshire Ripper.

FIONA   I'm not here to tell you that he is.

JUNE   'Now's your chance to get rid of your husband love.'
            That's how I hear you start it.
            Is that what you were gonna say to me? That your tactic?
            'Cept I made it all the easier for you, didn't I.
            Since you've been buttering me up all these months.

FIONA   I have not been buttering / you up

JUNE   Pretending to be my friend.

FIONA   It's not my fault you've none else!

JUNE   So what is it, hey?
            What – you seen his car in Chapeltown?
            You seen girls in his car?
            God you must be pretty bloody desperate.
            He lost his job and now he drives a taxi love.
            So yeah. You're gonna see some girls in his car.
            And d'you know he even gives some of them poor girls a free lift at night to keep 'em safe.

FIONA   We've got a tape.

JUNE   A tape?

FIONA   We got a cassette sent us at Millgarth.
            From him.

JUNE   –

FIONA   I'm telling you this in confidence.
            I shouldn't even say anything about this.

JUNE   –

FIONA   Dick Holland himself called me through to his office. Got me to transcribe the whole thing.
            I heard it. I heard it all. I heard his

            –

            This is a breakthrough.

JUNE   –

FIONA   Not even the squad know about it.

JUNE   –

FIONA   I was the one trusted to do it. Only me.
              My name shouted through the whole office and
              then it was me and
              him.
              Me and that voice. In that little room.
              I know every bit of it. Every syllable.
              The ways he finishes his sentences. The words he
              stumbles over.
              Every pause he takes.
              His breath.
              I can hear it in my head right now.
              –
              It's a Geordie.
              The Ripper's a Geordie.

JUNE   –

FIONA   A Geordie that drives a car at night.
              That can get across Pennines.

JUNE   Little Mrs Appleyard two streets down.
              Interviewed her husband. D'you remember? He
              drives a lorry for Newtons. That was it. That was
              all you had. But you roll up in all your sodding
              Splendour. Your fine fine uniforms. Little boys
              in blue.
              Knock knock fucking knock Mrs Appleyard!
              We'd like to ask your chap a few questions!
              Bold as brass, middle of the day. Not one ounce of
              respect for that poor lady. She had the whole street
              watching.

FIONA   Do you want him caught or not?

JUNE   Poor you Fiona poor you. How scary it must be
              standing on all those doorsteps. Talking to blokes
              like George Appleyard and Dennis Collier.
              Do they make you a brew and all, after your knees
              have stopped knocking?

FIONA   I am doing you a favour, coming here to you first.

JUNE   Mr Appleyard landed in hospital two month ago.
Took too many of his heart pills.
And even after that
Even after that
You know what they're saying?
No smoke without fire.

FIONA   Well that's very sad. That that happened.

JUNE   You've got teachers telling little kids to spy on
their dads.
You've got bobbies knocking on any old door to
see if someone's pissed off with their husband.
And you
You've got your little tape now.

FIONA   Look I'm interviewing Dennis either way. He's
from Newcastle. If not me then someone else will
eventually.

JUNE   But you got the scoop? Lucky girl.

FIONA   This is my job.

JUNE   What you want's the trophy though in't it. The
grand prize!
A Geordie in handcuffs. Any Geordie?

FIONA   You're becoming hysterical.

JUNE   I think I'd know if my husband was a serial killer.

FIONA   And that's what every wife says.
How can you ever know for sure, ey?

JUNE   Because I'm the one doing his FUCKING
LAUNDRY.

          –

JUNE   That man calling you into his office, asking for
you specially

FIONA   Dick Holland.

SHARON   Helen?

JUNE   Whoever he is

SHARON	Hi.
FIONA	Head of the investigation.
SHARON	Didn't know who else to call.
JUNE	That isn't a promotion, love.
SHARON	Would you get on a bus to Bradford?
JUNE	That doesn't make you a detective.
SHARON	I'll pay the fare.
JUNE	That makes you a fucking secretary.
	It pivots on a breath –
HELEN	What's with all these books?
SHARON	I swapped courses. Don't tell Mum.
HELEN	Can you do that?
SHARON	She'll think it's stupid.
HELEN	What?
SHARON	Women's Studies. That's what I'm doing, now. It's the first time it's been done in the whole country.
HELEN	Why d'you want to study women?
SHARON	It's like social and economics and political. It's all sorts.
HELEN	Sounds lezzie to me.
SHARON	We do that too actually.
HELEN	You gotta be a lezzie for your university?
SHARON	Ha-ha.
HELEN	I been to your Big Bop Boo-de-Wop. I seen 'em all at it.
SHARON	Mrs Big's Benefit Bop. You know I got interviewed about that. By the police.
HELEN	About your lesbo dance? Why about that?

SHARON   Cos we were raising money for the Leeds
           Women's Defence Campaign.

HELEN   So?

SHARON   They fucking hate us organising. It terrifies them.

HELEN   They shoulda come to dance. It wor me that wor
           terrified.

SHARON   Seriously though. They hate it.
           They're just obsessed with trying to find out who's
           in charge and they just find it totally terrifying that
           that's not how it works.

HELEN   What's not?

SHARON   It was funny actually. Here you'll like this
           It's a good joke.
           So they were just asking, over and over
           So come on then – who's Mr Big?
           And we're all saying – there is no Mr Big.
           Cos there isn't.
           And they roll their eyes and say – alright, who's
           Mrs Big then?
           As if THAT'S why we weren't answering the
           question!
           (*Laughs.*)

HELEN   ?

SHARON   Cos they can't understand a non-patriarchal form
           of hierarchy. It's totally beyond them that we
           wouldn't have a leader.
           With a penis.
           Or even without a penis.

HELEN   That's the joke?

SHARON   Well, yeah.

HELEN   No offence Sharon but you get less funny the
           cleverer you get.

SHARON   Well.
           Maybe it's cos I'm getting cleverer by learning
           more about the injustices of the world.

HELEN   Don't ever stop, you, d'you.

          –

HELEN   Ere you been listening to that tape they put out?

SHARON   I've heard it, course.

HELEN   I can't get enough of it, me.
          Wish I could hear the other bits.

SHARON   What other bits?

HELEN   The bits they left out.
          I heard from one of the girls they chopped it up
          and left some bits out. So that they know when
          they've actually got him. In case some weirdo
          tries to say that it's him when it isn't.

SHARON   Why would anyone pretend to own up to
          something like that?

HELEN   Cos there's some properly sick-in-the-head
          bastards out there Sharon.
          You wouldn't even know.

          –

          You know there's always a queue down phonebox.

SHARON   What?

HELEN   When the kids get let out of school. Busy times
          like that. There's always a queue to listen.

SHARON   To what? The tape?

HELEN   Cos they set up that phone line, din't they. That
          you call up and listen to it.

SHARON   There's a queue of people waiting to listen??
          God it's like we're all addicted to this
          fucking
          poison in us.
          What the fuck is wrong with us?!

HELEN   Calm down.

          –

SHARON   Did you hear there's a film coming into town.
          It's about a serial killer. Killing women.
          Killing prostitutes.

HELEN   Yeah?
          –

SHARON   Aren't you angry, Helen?
          Are you not angry about that?

HELEN   –

SHARON   We were talking about doing something about it.

HELEN   Who's we?

SHARON   I want to drive a car through the window. Right
          through it. The cinema.
          I've been thinking and I think I'd really like to just
          fucking put my foot absolutely flat on an
          accelerator and just explode through something.

HELEN   You wanna break glass so punch your mirror like
          a normal person.

SHARON   Nothing ever changed the world without breaking
          it first.

HELEN   You want to go down shops and get some cider?
          Calm down?

SHARON   You know some people think we should split the
          world in half. Have all the men living on one side,
          and all the women on the other.

HELEN   That's stupid.

SHARON   Some people think it's our duty not to be with men
          anyway.
          That we have like a moral imperative to be with
          women instead.

HELEN   What if you don't fancy 'em?

SHARON   I think you'd get used to it.
          Surely you don't fancy men. Not after all they've
          done to you.

HELEN   –

SHARON   Don't you ever wonder

HELEN   Wonder what?

            SHARON *grabs* HELEN*'s face.*

            Kisses her.

            What the fuck are you doing??

SHARON   I'm sorry!

HELEN   What the fuck you ask me to come here for. For
            this??

SHARON   Look Helen you're a prostitute I didn't think
            you'd mind so much.

            –

SHARON   I shouldn't have said that.

HELEN   Yeah well. You've um

SHARON   Helen I'm so sorry. That's not why I asked you

HELEN   I'm not your pet project you know.
            I'm not like your dog to teach tricks to.

SHARON   Helen I'm pregnant.

            –

HELEN   Are you.

SHARON   –
            I'm so sorry that I
            I dunno why I did that I just
            It's not an excuse.

HELEN   How long?

SHARON   Who's the stupid one now, ey?

HELEN   So… not a lezzie then.

SHARON   I'm not.
            I tried to be.

HELEN   Who the fuck *tries* to be??

–

That's nice, that is.

SHARON   What?

HELEN   Let's see your tummy then.

SHARON   –

HELEN   I wanna be a mum, me. But I reckon you should
have a flat first. Summat proper. I always think
you know
It's nice to be cared for, in't it. But it's nicer to
care.
Ah look you can see it I think.

SHARON   That's just chips.

HELEN   It's hard like. It's firm like a mum's tummy.
That's not chips that.

SHARON   I want to get rid of it.

HELEN   –

SHARON   I thought you might

HELEN   Get rid?

SHARON   Can you help me?

HELEN   –
Why me?

SHARON   I can't tell Mum.

HELEN   What about all those new friends of yours?

SHARON   I can't tell them I'm

HELEN   –
And why not?

–

SHARON   FUCK.
It's not meant to be like this.
I'm not meant to be like this.

HELEN   What you meant to be like then?

SHARON   I'm meant to be different.

HELEN   Better?
           Than who?

SHARON   –
           Do you know how?

HELEN   Course I know how.

           –

SHARON   What do I do?

HELEN   D'you mean?

SHARON   How do I…

HELEN   What?
           You mean like
           Can I get yous knitting needles? Gin in bathtub?

SHARON   Oh God

HELEN   Sharon! Fuck's sake.
           You just go doctor.

SHARON   Just the doctor?

HELEN   What d'you think??
           Course we go doctor.

SHARON   I didn't know.

HELEN   I'll come wi' you. S'not so bad.

SHARON   I thought I'd have to
           I've been imagining all sorts.
           That bit in *Alfie*.
           The bit in the kitchen.

HELEN   The one wi' Michael Caine?

SHARON   (*Nods.*)

HELEN   Sharon this is 1980!

SHARON   (*Sniffs. Starts to cry.*)

HELEN   And you don't even see owt.

SHARON   Really?

HELEN   No you just
You don't see owt, alright?

SHARON   (*Crying.*)
I'm sorry.

HELEN   You crying now?
Don't cry.

–

Come ere.

SHARON *goes to her.*

Silly mare.

HELEN *holds her.*

–

For what it's worth I reckon you'd be a nice mum.

SHARON   –

HELEN   You know it's up to you but
D'you not remember when you wanted to marry
Donny Osmond and have twenty kids?

SHARON   It wasn't ever twenty.

HELEN   Alright five then.
Can you still remember the names?
Jason and Jennifer

SHARON   The twins.

HELEN   Didn't you want to name one after that singer?

SHARON   Only if she was blonde.

HELEN   Blondie!
(*Laughs.*)
I thought that were brilliant, that idea.

–

HELEN   Look I'll do whatever. You know me. But
Just seems to me like it's not really you. All this.

SHARON   All what?

HELEN   Look there's some people in the world that can
          You know, that can do stuff. And I'm not saying
          you can't too, but
          You're only from Leeds, aren't you.
          What else you gonna do wi' your life, really?
          –

          And like, what's so wrong wi' your mum?
          I think your mum's great.
          If I were you

SHARON   What? What would you do if you were me?

                  Over the past four years

HELEN   I dunno Sharon. I'm not you, am I.

                  Over the past four years

          It just sort of feels like to me that
          over the past four years

                  Over the past four years

          it's like you've become a totally different person.

                  Over the past four years

SHARON   How many times do I have to say to you Helen.
          It's not me that's changed.

                  Over the past four years

          It's everything else.

              Sounds starts somewhere.

               And then it spreads.

        It comes from in front of us, and behind us.

             It comes from all around us.

           It surrounds HELEN and SHARON

              Presses in on all sides:

     Down from above, up from below, all around.

    Like water in a bathtub slowly drowning them.

*Over the past four years, ten women have been horribly
murdered and mutilated by a sadistic maniac: the Yorkshire
Ripper.*

Some of the victims were prostitutes.

Some were not.

*And now it seems that any woman in the wrong place, at the
wrong time can be a potential victim.*

How can we stop this madman from killing again?

Here's one way:
LISTEN.

*I'm not sure when I will strike again, but it will definitely be
some time this year. At the rate I'm going, I should be in the*
Book of Records.

Have you heard that voice before?

At work? Or in a pub? Club? On a bus, or in a queue?

Think.

Do you know somebody with a North Eastern accent like that?

A song plays:
'Thank You for Being a Friend' by Andrew Gold.

The track gets stuck:

'Thank you for being a
Thank you for being a
Thank you for being a'

*The sound of an engine; acceleration; glass shattering
at force.*

FIONA   Just take me through it step by step.

HELEN   I got in the car and then I drove the car to the
            cinema and then I put the car through the window
            in the cinema.

FIONA   Right.
            Just like that was it?

HELEN   Just like that.

FIONA   And you can drive a car can you Helen?

HELEN   Not well. Obviously.
         I put it through the fucking window.

FIONA   Not because you're a bad driver, I don't think.

HELEN   Cos.

FIONA   Right. 'Because' isn't really an answer for me, is it.

HELEN   Cos I'm angry.
         Cos
         Cos I've got more right to be angry than most.
         –
         Someone else told that to me. I didn't really get it,
         when she kept saying it.
         I kind of let a lot of stuff people say
         Let it slide right on over me like water in a bath.
         It's better that way. I reckoned that was better.
         I never thought I was allowed to be angry 'bout
         stuff. That's just your lot, in't it. You get born into
         your lot in life and it's just about getting on.
         I actually always figured in my stupid head that
         I'm doing an important thing, what I do.
         Obviously I'm not like what you do, I don't go
         round arresting people and protecting people but
         I actually do protect people.
         I actually do.
         Someone's got to be on the front line, don't they.
         And I always figured, I always thought
         These blokes. They're gonna do it any what way,
         aren't they.
         Council, you lot, Maggie down in London, they
         can say what they like
         But they're always gonna find a way to do what
         they want.
         Men like that. Men like him.
         Best we have a street for that. Best we have girls
         for that.
         I'm already a damaged person. Since a long time
         back.
         Why not let them do their damage here.

FIONA   Helen

HELEN   Please don't fucking cry.
             I'm really sick of people crying for me.
             You ever seen me cry?

FIONA   –
             I'm not crying.

HELEN   So that's why I done it.
             Been five years now.
             Someone's been killing us for five years now,
             ant he.
             And there's this film 'bout a
             Dunno. This film and they shouldn't be showing
             it, should they.
             It like... perpetuates the problem.

FIONA   Bloody hell.

HELEN   That's not mine that bit, I nicked that from
             someone else. I'm not that smart.

FIONA   I think you're pretty smart.

HELEN   Well I'm not.

             –

FIONA   I don't agree with what you said.

HELEN   What a fucking surprise a bobby dunt believe a pro.

FIONA   That's not what I mean.
             I think it will get better Helen.
             I think us lot, and council, and government – all
             them you reeled off. I think we're getting better.
             I think it will get better still.
             It's not always going to be like this.

HELEN   You think.

FIONA   I think it's changing now and I think it will change
             I mean it better, or they'll have me to answer to.
             –
             I think in fifty years' time things will be different.

HELEN   Like how?

FIONA   I dunno exactly.
            But better.

HELEN   Even for me?

FIONA   Especially for you.

HELEN   –
            Well
            fucking
            fingers crossed, ey.

FIONA   Helen I know you weren't the one driving the car.
            Why are you lying?

SHARON   I don't want to talk to you.

HELEN   Front line, aren't I.

SHARON   Why did they even let you in here?

HELEN   Why not?

            It pivots on a breath –

SHARON   I told them I didn't want to see anyone.

JUNE   –

SHARON   They're not allowed to do that. They're not
            allowed to just let people in.
            What sort of hospital is this.

JUNE   Janet's on reception.

SHARON   Of course Janet's on reception.
            Who the hell even is Janet?

JUNE   –

SHARON   Is there anyone in this sodding city you don't
            know?

JUNE   They let me in cos I'm your mother, Sharon.

SHARON   Yeah well I said no one.
            I didn't say no one except for mothers
            did I.

JUNE   I'll just sit quietly over here till you're done,
              shall I?

              –

SHARON   Where's Dad?

JUNE   Parking.

SHARON   Why did you not get the bus?

JUNE   Because I wanted to have a minute wi' you.

              –

SHARON   So what he's cross is he?

JUNE   He's just heard his daughter's off her legs
              He's worried. He's upset.

SHARON   What he's not cross that I put a car through
              a window?

JUNE   He's more concerned about how you are.
              We both are.

SHARON   (*Makes a noise.*)

JUNE   And whose car it was.
              And how much we're gonna owe 'em.

SHARON   Don't worry about that.

JUNE   Well Sharon

SHARON   Please Mum

JUNE   Someone's going to have to worry about it.

SHARON   Mum.

JUNE   We can't all just sail through life putting cars
              through windows without having to worry about
              the cost

SHARON   SHUT UP.

              –

SHARON   It was this rich woman I know from WAVAW.
              It was her car.
              And she knew what I was doing so

JUNE   She knew
            what?
            That you were going to have a crash?

SHARON   It wasn't a bloody accident, I'm not that bad of
            a driver.

            –

SHARON   Why d'you look so angry?

JUNE   Probably because I'm furious.

SHARON   Why? This has got nowt to do wi' you.

JUNE   Twelve weeks, Sharon?
            When were you gonna tell me?

            –

SHARON   How do you know?

JUNE   How long did you think you could keep it secret?

SHARON   That's illegal.
            That's
            patient confidentiality.
            You can go and get fucking Janet right now and
            bring her in / here

JUNE   When they called to say you'd had an accident,
            the doctor said not to worry
            Because both Mum and baby are fine.

SHARON   –

JUNE   Because most people might assume that a girl's
            mother knows when her daughter is pregnant.
            –
            Congratulations.

SHARON   –

JUNE   Am I to take it that this was some sort of Political
            Thing then?

SHARON   Don't say it like that.

JUNE   Like what?

            –

JUNE   I don't know what that cinema did to offend you
            so much Sharon but let me tell you, you're going
            to have to start thinking of things greater than
            yourself

SHARON   That's exactly what I was thinking about.

JUNE   now that you're a mother.

SHARON   I still don't know if I wanna be.

JUNE   Well I'm afraid that's out of your hands now.

SHARON   Still got another twelve weeks by my count.

JUNE   What are you talking about?

SHARON   –

JUNE   Sharon, no. You've no excuse to be doing that.

SHARON   You can talk.

JUNE   Excuse me?

SHARON   How many abortions have you been to?
            The way you go on about them it's like a check-up
            at the dentist.

JUNE   But those are vulnerable girls Sharon.
            Girls with no family, no support system. Girls
            without a house even.

SHARON   I don't own a house.

JUNE   –
            This isn't something to be making a point over.
            This is a baby.

SHARON   I'm not making a point.

JUNE   Unless there's something I'm not aware of that's
            happened to you.
            Is there something else that's happened, Sharon?

SHARON   –

JUNE   Then I think you've got to live with the
            consequences of your actions.

SHARON   I thought you were more forward-thinking than
           that.

JUNE   Then I'm afraid you thought wrong.

SHARON   As if you wouldn't have.
           If you'd had the option.

JUNE   –
           What?

           –

JUNE   Sharon
           I was desperate for you.
           How could you think that?

SHARON   We just don't get on really. Do we.
           Never really have.
           Have we.

           –

JUNE   I love you more than anything else in the world.
           I'm sorry if
           that's not always been clear.

           –

SHARON   I feel like I'm letting myself down.

JUNE   How's that?

SHARON   I wanted to be summat
           Extraordinary.

JUNE   You're already extraordinary.

SHARON   Different, I mean. I wanted to do things
           differently.

JUNE   Life has odd ways of throwing stuff at us. And we
           We've got a funny old habit
           Instinct, is maybe the better word
           of rising to the challenge. I think you'd find that in
           any woman.
           I think any mother would say the same, if you
           asked her how it happened. I wish we got our lives

            written out in a little book for us or a little script
            when we got born but that's not how it works.
            And no gain without pain, hey love?

SHARON   No pain without gain.

            –

JUNE   There's your dad outside. Shall I get him in?
            I said to him you'd already told me.
            That you were waiting on telling him till it was
            safe to.

SHARON   You already told him?

JUNE   It was him that answered the phone.

            –

            Well. We've got plans to make now, haven't we.
            Best get him in.

1979–1980

SHARON, FIONA, JUNE *and* HELEN
change their clothes.

SHARON *into something loose-fitting*
to hide the bump.

FIONA *into plain clothes.*

JUNE *removes her lanyard*
puts on a smock.

HELEN *grapples with an enormous bridesmaid dress.*

I'm Jack.

I see you are still having no luck catching me. I have the greatest respect for you George but Lord, you are no nearer to catching me now than four years ago when I started. I reckon your boys are letting you down George. They can't be much good can they? The only time they come near to catching me was a few months back in Chapeltown when I was disturbed. I warned you back in March that I'd strike again, sorry it weren't in Bradford. I'm not sure when I will strike again but it will definitely be some time this year. I'm not sure where. Maybe in Manchester. I like it there, there's plenty of them knocking about.

They never do learn, do they George? I bet you've warned them, but they never listen.

Well it's been nice chatting to you George.

Jack the Ripper.

Hope you like the catchy tune at the end!

'Thank You for Being a Friend'
plays.

It distorts.

Becomes grotesque.

ACT FIVE

HELEN What's this called?
I've never felt owt so soft in my life. Feel
Like a fucking queen.
Can you do my buttons up?

JUNE buttons her up.

How many are there?
Jesus must be hundreds back there.

Seeing in the mirror.

Wow.

Staring into the mirror.

Is that...
Is that really
Never knew I could look like that.

Smiling at the mirror.

I look like I'm in a cloud.
I look like I'm an angel.
I look like

SHARON brushes her hair.

You don't need to do that.
What you saying I haven't cleaned up proper this
morning?
D'you wanna do my teeth and all?

JUNE offers more adornments.

Nice.

SHARON applies them.

Done?

In the mirror.

Look at that.
Can't get enough of myself.
Look at that girl. Look at
Her.

–

So what d'you reckon?
Will I do?

SHARON *twirls her.*

Well go on then get me undone.
Can't stay in this clobber now can I.

JUNE *steps in.*

Wait just a second

In the mirror.

Just one more second…

JUNE *undoes the buttons.*

Oh.

The dress falls to the floor.

Yeah.

–

It is just me after all.

JUNE   There's no such thing as beginnings, Helen
            But this could be one. If you let it.

            It pivots on a breath –

HELEN   Are you sure?

JUNE   We'll get you the dress.
            It'll be a lovely day.

HELEN   But
            won't people like

JUNE   What?

HELEN   Dunno, might just think it's a bit weird, won't
            they.

JUNE   You know what Helen?
            Who cares what they think.

HELEN   Yeah.

JUNE   And it's nice to be able to give you a proper
            thank-you.

HELEN   For what?

JUNE   For taking the rap for Sharon.

HELEN   –

JUNE   You didn't think I knew about that?

HELEN   I shoulda stopped her anyway.

JUNE   Now we both know full well Helen
            that there's nothing in this world stopping our
            Sharon once she's set her mind to something.

HELEN   Yeah well.
            What's one more court date, hey.

JUNE   But thank you.

HELEN   She doesn't have to have me just cos of that.

JUNE   Of course it's not just for that.
            But who says you're not allowed a day to feel like
            a princess?

HELEN   –
            Never thought I'd ever be a bridesmaid.

            It pivots on a breath –

SHARON   Why not, hey?
            Why not you.
            Not the most normal wedding anyway, is it.

HELEN   Why not?

SHARON   Well it's just not the big church thing is it.
            Not with me being

HELEN   Can hardly tell

SHARON   Thanks.
            But it's not like I'm walking up an aisle.

HELEN   Why not?

SHARON   Cos we just have to get it done, don't we!

HELEN   Not very romantic.

SHARON   It'll be fine.
               It'll be nice.
               And it will be a bit romantic.
               I've written something.

HELEN   Ah yous big old softie after all!

SHARON   Here.

               A long silence.

               Would you like me to read it to you?

HELEN   –
               Nah.
               Don't spoil the surprise.

               –

SHARON   Michael wanted to do the honourable thing.
               And it's making my dad so happy.
               And anyway we talked about it
               If we don't fancy it after a few years
               There's always divorce these days, isn't there.

HELEN   If he hits you, you mean.

SHARON   I'm not expecting him to hit me!

HELEN   Then why?

SHARON   Cos I reckon it should be like a pretty basic like
               fundamental
               Like do you think I'd actually be marrying him at
               all if I thought he'd ever have a swing?
               He's not that sort of guy. Like not at all.

HELEN   I mean so why d'you think you'd get divorced
               then.

SHARON   I dunno. Life!
               Maybe we end up we don't like each other that
               much.

HELEN   Don't get you at all sometimes.

SHARON   It's just about having choices, isn't it.

HELEN   Is it?

SHARON   It's about being able to change your mind.

HELEN   –

SHARON   What?

HELEN   What?

SHARON   Your face has gone funny.

HELEN   Thanks.

SHARON   You know what I mean.

HELEN   Feel a bit funny actually.

SHARON   Why?

HELEN   Dunno I

SHARON   What's up?

HELEN   –
           Actually I
           think I've gotta go.

SHARON   Helen

FIONA   Helen? He's there.

SHARON   Helen, wait

FIONA   Can I give you a lift?

SHARON   Don't forget – it's two o'clock! A week on
           Saturday!

FIONA   Look like you're struggling a bit there.

           It pivots on a breath –

HELEN   Nah I'm alright thanks.

FIONA   That bag looks twice the size of you.
           Jump in.

HELEN	Don't get in cars with strangers.
FIONA	– Helen, you know me.
HELEN	I don't.
FIONA	You've never seen me out of uniform.
HELEN	What uniform?
FIONA	I'm PC Bainbrige. Fiona. Remember?
HELEN	Yeah sorry you look really different.
FIONA	Do I?
HELEN	Yeah.
FIONA	Really?
HELEN	– Yeah.
FIONA	Surely not that different. Face is still the same. Promise.
HELEN	Dunno. Just different. Just normal.
FIONA	Normal?
HELEN	Your tits look better though.
FIONA	– Thank you?
HELEN	Them blazers don't do owt for you.
FIONA	Yeah well. They weren't really made for us were they. It's just like a work skin though isn't it. It's just like slipping into a different version of yourself. Actually probably quite helpful, actually.
HELEN	For your tits to look shit?

FIONA	Actually, probably.
HELEN	Wouldn't do any good in my line of work.
FIONA	– Still making jokes I see.
HELEN	Why not.
FIONA	Where you headed?
HELEN	I got a uniform too.
FIONA	I'll drop you.
HELEN	Wear white. Catches the light good. Headlights.
FIONA	– You trying to wind me up? I'm offering you a favour here.
HELEN	Too easy, you. I'm alright thanks. Not too good for me to be seen in a car with a bobby.
FIONA	You didn't even recognise me.
HELEN	–
FIONA	That your bridesmaid dress?
HELEN	How d'you know?
FIONA	I'll be there you know. See you walking down the aisle.
HELEN	We're not having an aisle.
FIONA	Excited?
HELEN	Yeah. I suppose.
FIONA	I think it's a lovely thing that June asked you. She's always taken special care of you, hasn't she. And having Sharon make friends with you. She's a good woman, isn't she.
HELEN	– Yeah.

FIONA   What a day it'll be, hey? All her friends and
         family
         And having you as part of it.
         Walking down the aisle after Sharon.
         Says a lot to the kind of person June is.

HELEN   I said she's not having an aisle.

FIONA   It's a lovely statement. Her asking you to be there.

HELEN   Sharon asked me.

FIONA   Well of course, but June's always looked after you
         like / a daughter

HELEN   We're mates.

FIONA   Yeah, course you are.

HELEN   –
         So you going?

FIONA   Yeah I'll be there.

HELEN   You know Sharon?

FIONA   We've met a handful of times.

HELEN   Any others?

FIONA   What?

HELEN   Police. Just you, or more?

FIONA   I dunno. Just me, I think.

HELEN   Who else?

FIONA   What?

HELEN   Who else going?

FIONA   I don't know. Maybe like fifty-odd.
         Friends and family. It's a wedding.

HELEN   Who else going knows I'm a pro.

FIONA   –
         I don't know.

HELEN   –

FIONA   Can I give you a lift?
             Don't want to be getting that beautiful dress dirty.

HELEN   Yeah. No.

             –

             You take it.

FIONA   Alright. You coming?

HELEN   I'll get it off you later.

FIONA   Helen

HELEN   At the house or like
             I dunno take it to Mrs Collier.

JUNE   Hold on a sec!

HELEN   She'll look after it.

FIONA   Won't you be needing it?

JUNE   I'll be right with you!

HELEN   Yeah but
             Don't want it getting dirty. Like you said.

             It pivots on a breath –

FIONA   I ran into Helen down Armley way. She was
             lugging this down the road.

JUNE   Is that her dress?

FIONA   Asked me to drop it with you for safekeeping.

JUNE   She's meant to be meeting us at registry.

FIONA   Maybe she's meaning to get dressed there.

JUNE   Maybe.

FIONA   I'm sure you'll see her between now and then. You
             can ask her.

             –

JUNE   Not like you to be having a weekday to yourself.

FIONA   Nor you.

JUNE   Well I'm scaling back a bit.

FIONA   Oh?

JUNE   To be around a bit more. For all of them.

FIONA   Are we happy about that?

JUNE   Dennis certainly is.

FIONA   –

JUNE   Sharon's going back to finish her degree, part
            time. After the first year or so she reckons.

FIONA   That's good.

JUNE   Didn't realise I'd be doing it all over again.
            Not quite the same. Obviously. But

FIONA   Not the same at all.

JUNE   I'll be a nana this time.

FIONA   And totally different from when you was bringing
            Sharon up.
            I remember my mum just leaving the door wide
            open and I'd be playing in the street all day long.
            Wouldn't even think twice if I didn't show up for
            dinner, or if I showed up with two other kids for
            dinner.
            There'll be none of that any more.

JUNE   –
            You know I hadn't even thought.

FIONA   In't it weird now to think that we used to sleep
            with our doors unlocked?
            That were only five year ago.

JUNE   It'll go back to normal after he's caught though.

FIONA   D'you think?
            I reckon it might be different forever now.

            –

JUNE   What's with your day off then? Birthday or
            summat?

FIONA   I'm moving house.

JUNE   Unusually good of them to take summat like that
into account.

FIONA   I've taken a holiday. I'm moving back with my
folks.

JUNE   Oh?

FIONA   Me and Robbie ended it.
It's alright. I'm fine.
It's definitely for the best.

JUNE   D'you want to come in?

FIONA   No I'm alright. I've got another carload to do
actually. I should be heading.
It's absolutely the right decision. We weren't
seeing anything of each other anyway. Passing
ships in the night. And you know
Different dreams and that.
Everyone's getting married.

JUNE   –

FIONA   But I'm gonna be the first female detective in
West Yorkshire CID so

JUNE   You sure you want to have this conversation on
the doorstep love?

FIONA   –
Is Dennis in?

JUNE   You know he'll be at the wedding.

FIONA   But he'll be pissed then.

JUNE   Fair.

FIONA   I still think I did the right thing.
Every avenue's worth exploring.

JUNE   And I'll still disagree with you on that.

    –

JUNE   He's out right now.
You coming in for a cuppa tea?

A chaotic blend of
Music and
Voices and
Broadcasts and
Static.
Everything that we have heard before.

Snatches of the lyrics that we've listened to throughout
which are are first recognisable
distend, distort;
are mutilated.

The body of a prrrrrrrrrrrrr

Police renew the hunt for the man who has come to be known
as

an innocent, sixteen-year

Obviously now any woman out alone at night must be
considered

The body was in fact naked and it is a

Britain's most dangerous psychopath has indeed

Do you know somebody with a North Eastern

And now it seems that any woman in the wrong place, at the
wrong time

Some of the victims were

They never do learn, do they George?

Some were

I bet you've warned them, but they never listen.

SHARON   Feel like a bloody idiot.

JUNE   Now then

SHARON   What the hell was I thinking??
           Look at me I look like a fucking
           shepherdess.

JUNE   You look beautiful.

SHARON   You can see my tummy.

JUNE   Course you can't.

SHARON   You can.

JUNE   Course you can't.
Not with all that going on.

SHARON   Thanks. That makes me feel loads better.
–
What's happening? Where's Dad?

JUNE   With Michael. He'll come out in a minute.

SHARON   Shall I go say hi?

JUNE   No!

SHARON   Just feels a bit weird. Just waiting in here.

JUNE   That's what you're supposed to do.

SHARON   Should give him a wave at least.

JUNE   You'll be seeing him soon enough.

SHARON   –
What time is it?

JUNE   Five to.

SHARON   –
Where is she?

JUNE   I don't know love.

SHARON   I don't get it.

JUNE   Try not to think about it.

SHARON   I'm trying to think if I did something or
Like what the hell could I have done??
I asked her to be my bridesmaid.

JUNE   It was a lovely gesture.

SHARON   I could've asked anyone, but I asked her.
And now
I'm gonna have to do it alone.

JUNE   It's just a short walk love.
            You'll have your dad wi' you.

SHARON   You know what I mean.
            I thought it meant something to her.

JUNE   It does.

SHARON   Clearly not.
            I thought she loved that dress.
            Did you see her, when she had it on?
            Couldn't take her eyes off herself.

JUNE   It's my fault.

SHARON   What? No it's not.

JUNE   She wasn't ready for it.

SHARON   That's rubbish.

JUNE   I should've known.

SHARON   Stop acting like she's someone to be
            She's not like
            She's fine. She can turn up to a wedding and put
            a dress on.
            It's not that big of a deal.

            Music starts up.
            Aisle-type music.

            Well.
            That's my cue. How do I look?

JUNE   Very like a bride.

SHARON   Go on. You get in then.

            JUNE *leaves.*
            SHARON *waits.*

            Guess it's me on my own then.

            She sets off
            But before she reaches the end of the aisle
            We get to the reception.

            I always think it's a bit weird toasting your new
            life times like these cos

there's no such things as beginnings, really
Is there?
My mum, she always used to say
And I think it's a nice way to think about stuff
because
Putting a beginning on something sort of means
that there has to be an ending, somewhere.
So my mum, she says
You've probably all heard her say it some time or
another
'If you don't start summat, you'll never finish it.'
I figured it out, that, recently.
See it might sound like she's telling you to get
a shift on.
But actually, what it means is that most things –
they're just forever things.
Most life is just – happening, all the time.
–

It's all just sort of more like – one big, lovely,
muddle, isn't it?
Cos I don't know about you, but I've never moved
in straight lines.
Can't imagine I ever will but
Looking back
Sometimes
It's like we want to make them up.
This – this is the moment when life begins.
–

Sorry
I'll stop rambling on in a minute
But didn't want Michael to have all the glory.
Should start off on the right foot and know you've
got a wife that likes to talk, hey.
–

I heard something incredible the other day and it
sort of
Blew my mind, a bit.
This doctor told me, that when you're born
When a woman's born, she's already born with all
her children inside her. Obviously not like – fully
formed but

All the eggs in her ovaries, they're all already
there.
That those bits
Sorry if I'm grossing some of you out
That the ovaries are the first things to develop, in
a female fetus.
So all her potential, all those potential children,
they're born together.
And then – and this is when it gets a bit weird
So say you're pregnant with a girl
That girl inside, she's already got all of her
children inside her, as well.
It's like – you'd have all of your grandchildren,
already
Already there. In you.
Can you imagine?
Like halls of mirrors is what I think about.
Like those dolls that sit inside each other, going on
forever.
Infinite.
–

Dunno why I'm talking about this it just sort of
Haven't been able to stop thinking about it.
Them all in there and me out here and
We just all live through a lot more than we think
we do.
Don't we. If that's the case.
What we're carrying inside.
Cos now it feels like
I've got a hundred eyes looking out my eyes.
I've got thousands of hearts beating.
I've got millions of tongues desperate to be able to
speak
One day.
–

I was meant to have a bridesmaid here today.
I've known her since we were fifteen and she
turned up to sleep on my bedroom floor. You
probably already know
I'm sure you all have been talking about already
she's a girl my mum worked with.

Works with.
She um
She's not here
Obviously.
But I'd like to toast her anyway. Say thanks for
All the stuff I guess she's taught me.
Think I'd probably be a worse person for not
knowing her, even though you know
Though I think it was meant to be the other way
round.
–
Here's to Helen.

Static crackles
Fizzes
Rumbles

FIONA   You shouldn't be buying your own drinks. Not on
           your wedding day.

SHARON   It's fine.

FIONA   Let me get you one.

SHARON   Sort of ruined the mood didn't I.
           Not like everyone's ready to party now.

FIONA   I think it's the footie spoiling the atmosphere more
           than anything.

SHARON   I've heard people saying I'm twatted.

FIONA   Let them

SHARON   I'm pregnant, aren't I.
           That's the funny thing.

FIONA   –
           Right.

SHARON   So actually, I'm just a bit mental.

FIONA   It was probably just the hormones.

SHARON   Fuck off.

FIONA   –

SHARON   Sorry. I'm just kind of really sick of hearing about
           how I'm being remotely controlled by mystic
           forces. Bloody
           Hormones.

FIONA   Sorry.

SHARON   No I'm sorry I'm in a
           Christ this is my bloody wedding what's wrong
           with me.

FIONA   I really liked the speech.

SHARON   Give over.

FIONA   I thought it was sort of
           lovely. To think of.

SHARON   It is kind of insane, in't it?

FIONA   Mad. To think of all that going on
           inside.

SHARON   Actually makes me feel pretty powerful
           actually. Like I've got my own army
           inside.

FIONA   Well that's a scary thought.

SHARON   And like actually
           Yeah they can fuck us and enslave us and kill us
           all they like
           But can they do a thing like this?

FIONA   Not sure you need any other ammo than you've
           already got.

SHARON   I'll drink to that.

JUNE   Drink to what?
           What's in that?

SHARON   Gin. Rum.
           Vodka.
           Likkle splash of Coke to finish it off.

JUNE   Isn't she funny.

SHARON   Hilarious.

JUNE	Thanks for coming.
FIONA	Thank you for having me.
SHARON	Pleasure.
FIONA	Shame about Helen.
JUNE	We should get some dancing going.
SHARON	They'll not turn telly off till the footie's done.
FIONA	Did you ever see her after I bought the dress round?
SHARON	What? Why did you have her dress?
FIONA	Did your mum not tell you?
SHARON	Tell me what?
JUNE	I didn't want to upset you love.
SHARON	Tell me what??
FIONA	Calm down.
SHARON	I'm calm!
JUNE	She offered Helen a lift, that's all.
SHARON	What d'you mean? When?
JUNE	After the fitting I think.
FIONA	I drove by her walking down the road, swamped with this giant
SHARON	It's a garment bag. It wasn't that big.
FIONA	I only stopped to offer her a lift.
SHARON	So?
JUNE	We've not really seen much of her since.
SHARON	– Did you give her a lift?
FIONA	She didn't want one.

SHARON   No kidding she didn't want to get in back of
          another police car.

FIONA   I wasn't on-duty.

SHARON   So this was what
          This was

FIONA   Two weeks. Mebbe.

JUNE   Fortnight in't that long.

SHARON   Fortnight's long enough in Yorkshire, for
          someone like her.
          What d'you mean you've not seen her?

JUNE   She's just not been by the unit, that's all.

SHARON   That unusual?

JUNE   It's... not usual.
          Normally she'll stop by for her dinner, sometimes.
          Couple times a week or so.
          But not all the time.

SHARON   –
          You knew she wasn't coming today.

JUNE   I was hoping she would.

SHARON   What did you say to her?

FIONA   We just talked about the wedding.
          I only offered her a lift.

SHARON   –
          So
          what?
          –
          Do we like
          I mean
          Is she missing?
          Is she

FIONA   Not really.

SHARON   What's 'not really' mean?

FIONA   Means not really.
               We've no reason to believe

SHARON   Please don't gimme that

JUNE   Sharon, she's probably just
               Living her life.

SHARON   Right.

JUNE   She might've met someone.
               Gone to Huddersfield for a bit.
               Staying wi' one of her sisters.
               She might be sitting in another grotty flat with
               some new fella.
               She might just be

SHARON   This is her life.

FIONA   You never know wi' women like that Sharon.
               They're not reliable.

JUNE   We love her dearly but that's right love.
               She's unreliable.

SHARON   Actually. I'd say
               She
               Is probably one of the most reliable people you've
               ever met before in your life.

JUNE   You're getting silly.

SHARON   You said she's probably just – living her life.
               But *this* is her life.
               This was meant to be a new

               –

JUNE   What?
               What was it meant to be what?

SHARON   –

FIONA   We can't rescue her.

SHARON   Yeah we can.

JUNE   We can't, love.

SHARON   Yeah and what if she's

FIONA   She's not your damsel in distress.
           You're not Prince Charming come to save the day.

SHARON   What if she's next on the list?
           What if her face is on telly next?

JUNE   It's only two weeks.
           She'll pop up.

FIONA   You had to know that was always a possibility.

JUNE   Fiona

FIONA   You've been prepared for that.
           You know you have.
           You've been thinking the phone might ring since
           you was fifteen.
           You've been looking for her face on the news.
           We all have.

SHARON   That's not true.
           She's clever, is Helen.

FIONA   Clever's not smart though is it.
           And smart's not walking the streets
           When there's a Ripper in town.

           –

JUNE   Come on. What we doing?
           But this is your wedding day.
           We should be celebrating.

           Static crackles
           Fizzes
           Rumbles

           We should get some dancing going.
           Get some music on.
           Enough of the effing football.
           'Scuse me, can you stick the radio on?
           They'll have to deal with it I'm afraid.
           It is a bloody wedding after all.

Music.

*HELEN appears
in a bridesmaid dress.
A 1980s spectacle.
Pink satin and Bo-Peep frills.*

A man was detained in Sheffield

She starts to undress.

This man is now detained here in West Yorkshire

In her underwear, she tries very hard to

**He is being questioned in relation to the Yorkshire Ripper
murders**

But she can feel everyone watching her and

**It is anticipated that he will appear here before the court in
Dewsbury tomorrow**

She gets into a bath, still in her undies.

**I can tell you that we are absolutely delighted with
developments at this stage.**

Absolutely delighted.

*She lowers herself under the water, until she's fully
submerged.*

JUNE   There are no beginnings.

FIONA   There are no endings.

SHARON   But here's one.

          HELEN *explodes from the water.*

A Nick Hern Book

There Are No Beginnings first published in Great Britain in 2019 as a paperback original by Nick Hern Books Limited, The Glasshouse, 49a Goldhawk Road, London W12 8QP, in association with Leeds Playhouse

Cover artwork by Creative Arthur

Designed and typeset by Nick Hern Books, London
Printed in Great Britain by Mimeo Ltd, Huntingdon, Cambridgeshire PE29 6XX

A CIP catalogue record for this book is available from the British Library

ISBN 978 1 84842 886 7

Woodland
CARBON
www.woodlandcarbon.co.uk
NICK HERN BOOKS
Printed on Carbon Captured paper

www.nickhernbooks.co.uk

facebook.com/nickhernbooks

twitter.com/nickhernbooks